THE BUZZWORD DICTIONARY

THE BUZZWORD DICTIONARY

John Walston

Marion Street Press, Inc.
www.marionstreetpress.com

Cover and interior design by Gloria Chantell
Cartoons by Mark Hill
Author photo by Eileen Blass

ISBN 1-933338-07-5
Printed in U.S.A.

Marion Street Press, Inc.
PO Box 2249
Oak Park, IL 60303
866-443-7987
www.marionstreetpress.com

In memory of my Mom, Virginia C. Walston,
who nightly made me get up from the dinner table to
look up words I didn't know.

Introduction

From the beginning, let's get this straight. The BuzzWord Dictionary is meant to be fun — and hopefully a little educational.

But it's not the culmination of my life's work. And while it took me seven years to produce, I didn't slave alone for days on end in a dimly lit room pounding out what I hoped to be the definitive collection of buzzwords.

In fact, I seldom wrote more than one definition on any given day. And I had thousands of people helping me write the definitions.

I should explain.

You see, seven years ago my colleagues and I came up with this goofball idea of writing a BuzzWord dictionary to make fun of our CEO (name withheld just in case I need him for a future job reference). He was an intriguingly pompous sort who couldn't have a simple chat without spewing out a dozen buzzwords to describe his vision for the company.

Of course, after writing 75 definitions I realized that this book-writing thing was a lot of hard work and I didn't have that kind of time and energy. After all, I had two small children who thought Daddy shouldn't spend so much time in front of the computer.

So I created BuzzWhack.com, a Web site dedicated to poking fun at buzzwords, particularly business buzzwords, which seem to consume our lives.

Now here's the good part.

Since I didn't have the time to write a book, I thought I'd get BuzzWhack's readers to do it for me. So I asked them to nominate buzzwords that drove them nuts. Since BuzzWhack's inception more than 2,000 people have done just that, and the site has become a popular feature on the Internet with nearly 10,000 folks receiving BuzzWhack's daily email — BuzzWord of the Day.

Now more than seven years and hundreds of thousands of Web clicks later, The BuzzWord Dictionary is finally ready for the bookshelves.

I hope you enjoy it, and but most of all I hope you get a good laugh.

John Walston

THE BUZZWORD DICTIONARY

100% zero
An expression that emphatically states the ultimate negative. "The chances of this project succeeding are **100% zero**. It's just not going to happen."

10,000-foot view
Lofty synonym for "overview" used to overkill proportions by the media. Example: The **10,000-foot view** of the problem reveals the obvious. Also spotted: "the 33,000-foot view" and "the 40,000-foot view."

1K buffer
If a techie says you have a **1K buffer**, he's not talking about your computer — he's insulting you. It means you have a particularly low capacity for learning and remembering new things. "He's got a **1K buffer** when it comes to the new accounting software."

12:00 Flasher
A person of limited technical know-how. Giveaway: His/her VCR incessantly blinks "12:00."

2K6
The cool way of saying 2006. Gamers especially love it.

360-degree feedback/review

This is when you get it from all sides. It's the latest in performance evaluations. The victim, er, person is assessed by everyone who has regular contact with him/her — managers, subordinates, colleagues and customers.

404

A derogatory term used to describe someone who is totally clueless. "Don't bother asking Bill...he's **404**." Comes from the pesky error message you get when the Web page you're looking for can't be found: 404 Not Found. See *moved to Atlanta*

411

Thanks to Ma Bell, we have a new synonym for "information." As in: "I haven't got much time, so just give me the **411**!"

50-50-90 rule

A variation of Murphy's law. Given a 50-50 chance of things going right, they'll go wrong 90% of the time.

A2O
Shorthand for comparing dissimilar things — apples to oranges. "I'd disregard that. It was an **A2O** analysis."

abandonware
Any software, generally still protected by copyright, that's no longer sold or supported by the maker, but popular enough to be illegally "shared" by software pirates.

ABM
Anything (or Anyone) But Microsoft. A popular philosophy that reflects the backlash against the software giant's market domination and regularly promoted by technology vendors and consultants who make their living selling alternative (open source, Linux, Unix, etc.) solutions.

academic junk food
College courses with absolutely no value other than being an easy way to get an A.

across the aisle
Originally the "aisle" between Republicans and Democrats in Congress, it now applies to anyone with an opposing viewpoint. Example: "Management thinks we should focus on becoming profitable, but our investors **across the aisle** think we are due for an IPO."

action items
A term that sounds more macho and businesslike than "to do" list.

actionable
A legal term that's been co-opted by marketers, consultants and techies. In the legal world, it's "giving cause for legal action," such as a lawsuit. Now it's anything you can act on. "After analyzing your production line, we recommend these four **actionable** steps."

ADAM
Acronym for Androgen Deficiency in Aging Males, but better known as "male menopause." While not nearly as nasty as the female version, it lasts a whole lot longer — up to 40 years — which probably explains why there are so many cranky old men. Also known as *andropause*.

administrivia
On a Web site, it's the odds and ends that don't quite fit under a specific category or merit their own page. Frequently it's the legal stuff about copyrights, liability, licensing, etc. You know, all that administrative stuff. Privacy issues used to be **administrivia**, but with the growing concerns about security, that topic now rates prime time display.

advermation

Some see this as the more evil twin of infotainment. **Advermation** is advertising that presents itself as information and tends to downplay or even disguise the fact that it's trying to deliver a marketing message. In most cases, it's a simple Web page that is blurring the lines. Conspiracy theorists, however, offer up examples like this: An ABC television "film critic" delivers a glowing review on the evening news and shows the new release's promotional trailer. The movie is from Disney, ABC's parent company. Hmmmmmmmm.

affluenza

The affliction of being too focused on buying material things, working too much (and still not having enough money), and stressing out about all of it.

agreeance

A bastardization of "agreement." Created by the BuzzMakers because it sounds more important and "official." It's now bandied about at business meetings and is often buried in the fine print of Web site privacy statements. "All parties are in **agreeance** . . ."

agritainment

Farm-based tourism. Includes family-style activities, such as corn mazes, haunted hay rides, pick-your-own pumpkins, etc. This growing phenomenon gives city slickers a taste of rural life while helping farmers diversify their revenue stream.

air cover

Borrowed from the military, it's when someone in upper management agrees to take the flak for an unpopular decision — while you do the dirty work. "The CIO will provide **air cover** while you make the cuts to reduce costs."

all cotton

In basketball, it describes a shot that swishes through the net without hitting the rim. "And Allen Iverson shoots ... it's **all cotton**!" Also: *Nothing but net.*

All Flash, No Cash

The financial version of "All Talk, No Action" and "All Hat, No Cattle."

alpha geek

The most technically proficient person in a group or company.

alpha pup

A term used by market researchers for the "coolest kid in the neighborhood." "If the **alpha pups** like it, we'll sell a million of 'em."

alt-tab

It's more than just a key on your PC, it's the latest way to save your job. Hitting "alt+tab" on your keyboard will hide the window that's on your screen and bring up one from behind. It's used frequently in the workplace to

PR-babble

Excerpt from a real press release:

Verbiage, Inc. is the worldwide leader in unified collaborative communications (UCC) that maximize the efficiency and productivity of people and organizations by integrating the broadest array of video, voice, data and Web solutions to deliver the ultimate communications experience. Verbiage's standards-based conferencing and collaboration are supported by an open architecture and they integrate seamlessly with leading telephony and presence-based networks. With its market-driving technologies, best-in-class products, alliance partnerships, and world-class service, Verbiage is the smart choice for organizations seeking proven solutions and a competitive advantage in real-time communications and collaboration.

hide the fact that you've been surfing the Net, instead of doing that report the boss wanted. "I didn't finish reading that joke you emailed me; my boss walked by so I had to **alt-tab**."

Amazon-ized
That sick feeling you get when you wake up one morning and find your industry being dominated by a Web-based retailer.

ankle biter
A small cap stock. "When I bought the stock it was an ankle biter. Now the company is in the Fortune 1000."

anonymize
A member of the enormous "ize" family. Not terribly imaginative, it means "to make anonymous." It's an old trick of the BuzzMakers: Take a noun, add "ize" and turn it into a verb. "We **anonymized** the customer responses before putting them on the Web."

anticipointment
The feeling you get when a product or event doesn't live up to its own hype. "Windows ME was a huge **anticipointment**."

AOS
All Options Stink. Taken from the military, but easily applied to politics, business, etc.

architect (as a verb)
Mutilation of a noun by the "computer architecture" world. "Tell us what you want your system to do and we'll **architect** it for you." What's wrong with the word "design"?

ASCII babe
A celebrity or well-known personality who has been sophisticatedly illustrated using nothing but ASCII characters. See examples at www.asciibabes.com

associates
Thanks to companies like Wal-Mart, corporations no longer have "employees" — they have **associates**. Of course, they're still paid like employees.

asteroid event
Any major news or event that pushes a company to the brink of extinction by wiping out the value of its stock almost overnight. The corporate version of what killed the dinosaurs.

astroturf
A phony grassroots effort in which lobbyists and special interests flood politicians, particularly members of Congress, with email in an attempt to sway their opinions. The tactic, however, has backfired since members of Congress have pretty much given up on trying to read the 80 million email messages they receive each year.

Atkinsed

To lose weight using the Atkins Diet. "I have recently **Atkinsed** myself down to a size 12." Also: A marketing ploy to take advantage of the Atkins Diet craze. Burger King **Atkinsed** its menu, which simply meant it would sell you the burger without the bun.

ATNA

All Talk, No Action. Acronym describing a person who makes promises with great fanfare, but seldom follows through. See *All Flash, No Cash*

audio caffeine

High energy, stimulating music that gets you moving in the morning.

auditability

Corporate-speak describing the likelihood of information to withstand an auditor's scrutiny. "We have assessed its **auditability** and it should pass SEC muster."

automotive acne

The collection of broken headlights, crumpled panels and bent fenders that identifies a car as belonging to a teenage driver.

back-sourcing

When outsourcers fail to deliver quality, service or cost effectiveness, companies will bring the job back in house. As in: "It's time to **back-source** this one, because we've lost control of what we're doing."

bad cosmetics

A favorite at Enron. Any action or practice that would reflect badly on the company. Enron memos noted that there was great concern about "**bad cosmetics** being aired publicly," particularly in The Wall Street Journal. Outside the corporate world, it's known as "dirty laundry" or "dirty linen."

BAFO

Business acronym for Best And Final Offer.

baked in

Corporate-speak for "included." "The shipping costs are already **baked into** the list price."

bake-off

Contest where competing vendors submit their products for head-to-head performance tests in hopes of winning the customer's business. "We had seven vendors in the **bake-off**."

B original? 4get it!

"Business-to-business" was too traditional sounding. B-to-b was too clunky. **B2B** is way-cool and much easier to work into headlines and ads. But not all businesses cater to other businesses, so **B2C**, business-to-consumer, was born. But wait, some companies serve companies that serve consumers. What are they called? **B2B2C**, of course! Another huge customer is the government, thus **B2G**. What if you serve all those markets? Then you're **B2A** (business-to-anybody) or **B2E** (business-to-everybody).

bandwidth (as applied to people)

Technology truly has permeated our lives when we start applying tech terms to people. "So, what's your personal **bandwidth** like?" Expect to hear it from your boss soon. It means: How much extra time do you have to take on new projects?

barcode rape

When trade show "booth bunnies" grab you by the name tag and swipe the barcode (to earn a commission) before even talking to you about the products or services they offer.

barn raising

Borrowed from a simpler time, it means to solve a difficult problem by pulling staff and resources from the four corners of the company to develop a solution. "We'll need to do a little **barn raising** to solve this one." The term IS more palatable than "multi-functional task force."

Barneyware

The purple dinosaur may have faded from the scene, but his legacy lives on. **Barneyware** is anything that has little or no substance. Example: A joint press release by two companies that have nothing new to announce, but in order to generate media attention declare their mutual admiration for each other. In effect, the release says nothing more than "I love you, you love me, we're a happy family."

barrybonds
Financial instruments that have an impressive growth rate, but also a high risk factor. Named for baseball star — and reputed steroids abuser — Barry Bonds.

BAU
Even old standbys can become acronyms. This one is the much bandied about corporate term for "business as usual."

BDN
A Big Damn Number. Frequently used by sales and marketing types to emphasize value. For example, a $5,000-a-month savings isn't nearly as impressive as the annual **BDN** — $60,000.

Bear Market Depressive Syndrome (BMDS)
A medical term for the overwhelming sense of inadequacy, shame and regret you feel whenever the stock market takes a dip. Coined by Dr. John W. Schott, an author, practicing psychiatrist and portfolio manager for Steinberg Global Asset Management.

bee break
Sneaking off to the bathroom in the middle of dinner to check email on your BlackBerry.

beer googles

Searching the 'Net while intoxicated. Comes from the phrase "beer goggles," which refers to the fact that every woman is attractive to a drunk man.

beggarware

Any free software, generally downloaded from the Internet, whose author "begs" for a donation to help support continued development.

belly buttons

The Web world counts eyeballs. The insurance and managed care industries count **belly buttons**. One person equals one **belly button**. So an insurance policy that covers five **belly buttons** covers five individuals. The managed care folks say, "That program impacts 3 million **belly buttons**."

Below Zeros

This is a marketing term, not a temperature. They're customers who cost more to serve than they return in value. Example: A customer who ties up a salesperson for 45 minutes while trying on 14 pairs of Gucci shoes, then buys a six-pack of tube socks for $1.98, complains about the price and walks out. Also known as **BZs**.

bench

"We've got **bench**," the salesman assures the customer who wants to know if the company can deliver as promised. "We need **bench**," complains the manager whose department has been running two down for the past six months. In other places, **bench** is the justification for an excessive number of excessively-paid executives sitting in gargantuan offices.

best of breed

One of the top honors at the Westminster dog show, but in the tech world it's supposedly the top software or hardware in its class.

betamaxed

What happens when the "best" technology loses out to lesser technology in the marketplace. Coined during the VCR wars when VHS became the standard over the "superior" Betamax format.

BFO

Blinding Flash of the Obvious. "Jack is having another one of his **BFO** moments."

BHAGs

Big Hairy Audacious Goals. A **BHAG** gets people's creative and competitive juices flowing. Coined by authors James Collins and Jerry Porras, but now a favorite of pricey consultants.

BHNC

Big Hat, No Cattle. Another way of saying "All Talk, No Action." See **ATNA**

Big Uglies

Stocks with no sex appeal. Tech stocks are hot, but no one's touching the Big Uglies, such as Rust-Belt manufacturers, mining companies, etc.

bio break

Meeting-speak for "bathroom break." "Let's take a short **bio break** before moving on to action plans." Of course, coffee is served during such breaks at business conferences, resulting in the need for more **bio breaks**.

biocolonialism

The taking of knowledge and biological resources from an indigenous people without compensation. Frequently practiced by drug companies, which have discovered that some medical remedies of "primitive" tribes are far more effective (and profitable) than those produced by modern science. Also known as *biopiracy*.

BIRGing

Sports psychology term to describe how fans boost their own self-esteem by Basking In Reflected Glory of their favorite team. It makes fans paint their faces in team colors, secretly listen to games during work, and spend a small fortune buying team logo-laden apparel and goofy-looking bobbleheads.

bi-tonal

1) For those of you who haven't figured it out, the **bi-tonal** menu choice on your fancy, super-duper copiers, printers and scanners means black and white. 2) Describes old-style managers. A person who only sees it two ways — his way or the highway. Also, a manager who sees things as right or wrong and leaves no room for discussion.

BlackBerry thumb

Swelling or pain at the base of the thumb, generally suffered by execs or wannabe execs from operating their BlackBerrys.

black-collar workers

Once a term for miners and oil workers, today it more often refers to creative types (artists, graphic designers, video producers) who've made black attire their unofficial uniform.

blahger

A blogger whose message primarily consists of blah-blah-blah.

blaired

To have one's work stolen or copied. Refers to former New York Times reporter Jayson Blair's penchant for stealing the work of other journalists.

blalker
Someone who uses a blog to stalk or hound another individual.

blame shift
To deflect responsibility by pointing the finger at someone else.

blamestorming
A group process where participants analyze a failed project and look for scapegoats other than themselves.

blanding
Branding schemes that strip out any uniqueness in a corporate identity in order to appeal to a larger audience. The resulting look: bland.

bleg
To use one's blog to beg for assistance (usually for information, but occasionally for money). One who does so is a "blegger."

blix
To look without seeing. A reference to Dr. Hans Blix, the U.N.'s chief weapon's inspector. "They **blixed** the area and didn't spot a single violation."

bloated syntax
Anything that's overwritten — often padded with unnecessary adjectives or laden with hyperbole. Also appropriately known as "BS."

bloatware

Software that has more features, buttons and capability than you'll ever need. It eats up storage space on your drive and hogs memory in order to run. The result of bad or simply lazy design.

blocking and tackling

The basics or fundamentals. Another example of business folks using sports terms and analogies (football in this case) to make themselves clear — even though the message is missed by those who don't follow sports. "First we need to get back to **blocking and tackling**, then we can discuss advanced strategies and techniques."

blogives

Web log archives. (Somewhere in the million blogs that fill cyberspace, there must be something worth saving for posterity.)

blogna sandwich

When employees spend their time reading blogs during their lunch breaks.

blook

A book that began as a blog until someone figured they could make money off it if they published the same stuff on paper.

BLOW

Been Laid Off Work.

Bluetooth fairy

Someone who spends his or her day with the blinking glow of a Bluetooth headset plugged into one ear.

BMWs

Bitchers, Moaners and Whiners. "We'd get a lot more accomplished if we didn't have so many **BMWs** working here."

bobbleheading

The mass nod of agreement by participants in a meeting to comments made by the boss, even though most have no idea what he just said.

BOBFOC

Body Off Baywatch, Face Off Crimewatch.

bobos

Short for Bourgeois Bohemians, a confounding mingle of 1960s rebellion with 1980s ambition. Coined by author David Brooks. Bobos drink coffee because it stimulates mental acuity, but shun booze because it dulls the senses. They will go to the beach in the skimpiest of bathing suits, but are astonished if you neglect to put on sunblock to prevent cancer. And driving your SUV without a seatbelt is positively immoral.

BOBBLEHEADING

Bode, Bode-ed

To waste an opportunity. Reference to an overhyped, over-exposed Bode Miller who partied his way through Torino and literally **Bode-ed** the entire Olympics.

BOGOFF

Sounds like an insult, but it's simply a marketing gimmick used to boost sales volume, or in some cases to get consumers to try a product because it's such a great deal. Translation: Buy One Get One For Free.

BOHICA

An acronym muttered by the people who do the real work when senior managers announce their latest and greatest sales/customer service/quality initiative. It's more polite than Bend Over, Here It Comes Again.

boiling the ocean

The result of working hard without focus or purpose. "All she's doing is **boiling the ocean**." Also known as "spinning your wheels" and "running in place."

bolt-on acquisition

Describes a product or company acquisition that fits naturally with the buyer's existing business lines or strategy.

Boolean Approach

A decision-making process favored by business execs in which the answer is either "yes" or "no." Also known as a "digital decision."

borking

To vilify or defame someone. Originally coined after Robert Bork's U.S. Supreme Court nomination was torpedoed in 1987 and refers to opposition to a judicial nominee for purely political reasons. Today **borking** has morphed to include anyone who gets trashed in the media.

born digital

Documents (books, manuscripts, reports, etc.) not published on paper. They are created on a computer and distributed electronically.

botchulism

Quick-fix solutions or business practices that turn toxic. "Arthur Andersen had a bad case of **botchulism**. It crippled the company and killed my 401K."

bot herders

Computer hackers who specialize in hijacking personal computers connected to the Internet using bots (programs that run automatically). Bot herders then use them in unison to send spam, launch attacks on Web sites they don't like, etc.

bracket envy
The emotion that results when your last team in the Final Four office pool is eliminated while your colleague across the aisle still has three teams remaining.

bragability
The right to brag based on accomplishments. "Having competed in the Ironman has a high **bragability** factor."

brandalism
It's the "defacing" of schools, libraries and other public spaces with company logos, advertisements and corporate slogans. Remember when buildings were named after people we admired?

brandroid
Someone (usually a marketer) who relentlessly trumpets the brand and pushes for all decisions to be aligned with the company's "brand essence."

brandstorming
The process of brainstorming a new branding strategy.

brown bag session
A meeting scheduled during lunch hour in which the employee not only has to work but must bring his or her own lunch.

BSOD

Better known as the Blue Screen of Death. If you used the old versions of Microsoft Windows, you've probably met the **BSOD**. It's what happened when Windows didn't like something you'd just done, so it freaked out and gave you a bright blue screen and instructions on what to do. If you were lucky, those instructions ended with the words "To continue, hit any key."

BTA

Used to mark both the time before September 11, 2001 and how views have changed since. Something that is **BTA** would be considered naive and self-centered, and reflect attitudes held "before the attacks."

bubble up

The act of letting an idea or issue rise up the organizational chart to a superior. "The best ideas are the ones that **bubble up** from front line employees."

buck-rake

To hold a political fund-raiser. "He skipped the debate in order to **buck-rake** for his campaign."

budget dust

Year-end money that must be spent before it is swept away by the cold winds of a new fiscal year.

budget flush

The "use it or lose it" spending spree that occurs near the end of the fourth quarter. The last-minute draining of the budget is such a common practice by IT departments that Wall Street analysts factor it into their technology stock projections.

budgetunity

An "opportunity" for innovative budgeting. Used to put a positive spin on Michigan's budget crisis several years back. "The shortfall in revenue has given the governor a **budgetunity**."

bulletize

To highlight supposedly key information using bullet points. "To help explain my idea, I've **bulletized** the main points on the next slide..." Often used by people who can't explain themselves in complete sentences.

BUM

Interestingly, there are a lot of "business unit managers" in the corporate world, but the only folks who use the acronym are employees.

by the drink

How most bars dispense alcohol. In the Internet content world, it means to sell articles or information by the individual piece.

BYOA

Bring Your Own Advil. Description for a task that's sure
to give you a headache. "We need to install that
software on the Unix server — **BYOA**."

calendarize

The process of adding meeting details to a calendar, also known as scheduling. "Among the duties of the executive assistant will be to **calendarize** meetings for the CEO."

cantenna

A low-tech, home-made antenna constructed from tin cans and other handy components and used to increase the range of a high-tech, Wi-Fi (wireless) network.

capitalized reputation

A company's value based on name recognition and brand, not tangible assets. Or as Alan Greenspan put it: "The rapidity of Enron's decline is an effective illustration of the vulnerability of a firm whose market value largely rests on **capitalized reputation**. Trust and reputation can vanish overnight. A factory cannot."

capsizing

Downsizing gone awry. It's the process of a company repeatedly reducing head count, but not the work, until it goes under.

carbeque

For commuters, it's a rush-hour vehicle fire that ties up

traffic for hours. For dieters, it's a low-carb meal cooked on the patio grill.

cardboard crack
A reference to "Magic: The Gathering" and other trading card games for kids, and their addictive nature. Could also be applied to baseball cards.

C the Buzz

The letter C, as in chief, is big in buzzdom. There's **CXO**, which can be generically applied to any exec, from the CEO to COO. Then there's **C-level**, which refers to all of a company's senior execs. "To sell that, we'll have to reach **C-level** people." They all office on the top floors of headquarters, AKA the **C-suite**. Always try to avoid a **C-gull**, which is a **C-level** executive with the annoying habit of swooping in and out of meetings and leaving a huge mess for his/her subordinates to clean up. If a **CXO** fails to get the job done, it might be time for a **C-change**.

carpool couture
Designer label fashions priced for working moms.

carried a bag
A seasoned outside salesperson who has traveled extensively, been responsible for meeting a large quota and has the ulcers to prove it. "All of our sales consultants have **carried a bag**."

cell phone manager
Someone with a total lack of project management skills. He/she spends all day on the cell phone calling people and asking stupid questions.

cellcert
The 30-year practice of holding up your Zippo or Bic lighter during a concert is finally fading. Today's fans hold their camera cell phones high, snapping photos and letting friends back home hear — and see — the concert.

cellevision
TV delivered through your cell phone.

cellopain
The crass idiot who talks loudly and obliviously on his cell phone in a public place.

cellular Macarena

The dance that occurs when a cellular phone rings in a public place. Everyone reaches for their coat pocket, front pants pocket, back pants pocket, etc.

centergistic

Focusing on one main goal or purpose. "We need to keep this meeting **centergistic** if we're going to make our deadline."

channibalism

When a new marketing channel steals business from existing channels without adding new growth. While this is a legitimate business concern, it's downright frightening to the executive whose bonus is tied to the old channels.

chatterati

The talking heads, pundits, columnists, talk show hosts, etc., who have something "expert" to say on every issue — whether it's meaningful or not.

chimping

The "ooooh! ooooh!" sound made by a photographer when she spots a good photo while reviewing the images on the back of her digital camera.

China Syndrome
Business-speak for relocating manufacturing operations to China to reduce labor costs. Jane Fonda fans may remember it also means a nuclear reactor meltdown.

Chinglish
A combination of Chinese and English. Given the growth of China's economy, some folks think Chinglish will become the next global language.

Cingular merge
The jerky, zigzagging attempt to merge into a new lane of traffic by a driver with one hand on the wheel and the other on his cell phone.

circling the drain
What a struggling company does just before it goes down the tubes. "Jackson knew the company was **circling the drain** when he jumped ship."

clicks and mortar
Probably the real winners of the Internet Revolution: Traditional companies that managed to successfully integrate the Internet into their existing channels.

clicks-for-chicks
This one's not about the poultry industry. It's a reference to adult sites.

client-centric

Marketing-speak for anything that focuses on the needs of the customer. "We've boosted profits 30% since we began using a **client-centric** business strategy." Translation: We're making more money now that we're actually giving customers what they want. Brilliant.

climate sensing

A random survey of workforce attitudes. Generally done by walking around and chatting with the employees. Also known as *taking the pulse*.

CLM

A three-letter abbreviation making the rounds: Career Limiting Move. It refers to any incident that puts a roadblock in your career path. "Jack forgot to pick up his boss at the airport. It was a major **CLM**."

clockroaches

Employees who spend most of their day watching the clock instead of doing their jobs.

clueful

In the techie world, it's the opposite of clueless. "I'll get the answer as soon as I can find someone **clueful** at Network Solutions."

clustomer

A group or cluster of customers who have similar buying habits, tastes or needs.

CNN effect
The impact of live, ongoing TV coverage of news events — particularly on military operations or government policy. Thanks to 24-hour coverage and satellite technology, viewers often find out what's going on at the same time as the commanders and the politicians.

coachable moment
An opportunity to give on-the-spot, real-time feedback to an employee who just screwed up.

coaster
The result when your attempt to "burn" a CD fails. "I've made more **coasters** than music CDs."

COB
Acronym for "close of business," generally pronounced C-O-B, not "cob." "I need that report **COB** (by close of business today)." Also *EOB* — end of business.

cobweb site
A Web site that hasn't been updated in ages. The information is outdated, the links are broken, and it's figuratively growing cobwebs. Meanwhile, the owner likely is still being charged a monthly fee to have the site hosted.

cockroach
An apparently small problem that, when discovered, leads to many other problems.

codify

Consulting gurus "codify" information when they arrange it and write it down. Hopefully so it makes sense. "We'll **codify** the strategic issues for you." We've seen a lot of what consultants produce and we wonder if they aren't using the "other" meaning of codify: To reduce to a code.

coin-operated

Description of someone whose sole motivation is money. "He's a **coin-operated** salesman. He won't even call his mother unless it pays a commission."

cold eyes review

A review or evaluation of a proposal or project by someone who is unfamiliar with the subject matter.

Columbo site

The Web page that opens after you unsubscribe from an email list, where a final appeal is made to keep you. Named after TV detective "Columbo," who always had one last parting shot just as he turned to leave.

column fodder

Often pointless data entered into a spreadsheet to make it look more in-depth than it really is. "Columns A through C are the only columns that matter. The remaining 17 are column fodder."

coma factor

The degree of dullness of a meeting, presentation or reading material. "So let's try to describe this issue in language with a low **coma factor**."

compensated endorser

Term used to obfuscate that celebrities promoting a product are being paid to do so. Also used as a disclaimer: "I love that software — and no, I'm not a **compensated endorser**."

computerate

Computer literate. To understand how a computer works. "Are you **computerate**? Or do you need me to install that software for you?"

congestion pricing

The attempt to control traffic flow on toll roads by raising prices during peak periods, offering cheaper rates to cars that use toll tags, or giving discounts to cars with more than two passengers.

contact coordinates

Name, address, telephone number, email address, etc. "Give me your **contact coordinates**." See *personal coordinates*

content toxicity

Consultant-speak for out-of-date content. Considered poison for any Web site.

CORRIDOR WARRIORS

conversate

To have a conversation. Created by those who (for some bizarre reason) don't think "converse" or "talk" is adequate.

co-opetition

The result when two competing companies with overlapping products or technology find it beneficial to work together — ultimately increasing sales for both companies. Not to be confused with collusion.

corbesity

Corporate obesity. When companies become too big. They become fat and complacent. They get lazy, lose their creativity and are no longer able to move quickly in the marketplace.

CORFing

A sports fan's attempt to maintain self-esteem when his or her team loses by Cutting Off Responsibility for Failure. The loyal fan often CORFs by blasting the coach or a beloved player on the local sports talk radio show. See also **BIRGing**

corked

To initially appear flawless only to explode in your face later. "The project failed because someone **corked** the data." Inspired by Sammy Sosa's corked bat.

corporate anorexia
A company's unhealthy obsession with cutting the fat. Instead of producing a "lean and mean" operation, the single-minded focus on cost-cutting frequently creates a death spiral resulting in bankruptcy.

corporate antibodies
The forces inside a corporation that shield the company from unnecessary risk. In their zeal to protect the status quo, they often perceive new ideas and ventures as threats, thereby stunting the company's growth.

corporate DNA
A company's core values, culture, personality, etc., that supposedly get passed along to all new employees. **Corporate DNA**, however, is actually altered slightly every time a new person is hired. And a wholesale shift can occur simply by replacing the CEO.

corporateer
One who makes commerce a priority over culture. "The **corporateer** doesn't care what children learn, only what they buy."

corridor warriors
Employees and execs who spend their day racing from meeting to meeting, tethered to laptops so they can retrieve even the most basic information, take notes, and remain linked to the rest of the world via email. Also called *corridor cruisers*.

costification
To justify the cost of something, particularly a frivolous expenditure.

COTU
Center Of The Universe. Often used to describe people who are unable to see another point of view because wherever they're standing is the center of the universe.

counter-Googling
For years, folks have used Google to do background checks on people they're dating. Now businesses are "Googling" customers to dig up info to personalize their service and better target their marketing. "I **counter-Googled** all the new customers so we can send the right mailing to each."

CPB
"Conducting personal business" during office hours. Includes surfing the Net, speaking to your accountant, sending personal email, etc. "The project isn't complete because Jack has been **CPBing** all day."

crackberry
Another name for the BlackBerry that refers to its addictive nature and the inability of its users to focus on anything else for more than 10 seconds.

cranial prosthesis
A wig.

credenza-ware

An organization's strategic plan that is displayed prominently behind an executive's desk, but sits untouched until it's updated the following year.

CRM

Consultants say this stands for Customer Relationship Management software, but everyone else says it means Consultants Raking in Millions, since consultants seem to be the only folks financially better off after a company implements a CRM solution.

crop dusting

Surreptitiously passing gas while walking through a cube farm (an office full of cubicles).

crowdsourcing

Instead of outsourcing work to places like India or China, some innovative companies are crowdsourcing — using talent (generally cheap or free) that's scattered (not located in one place). Thanks to the Internet, a programmer in Boise with a few extra hours in his day can work for a Pennsylvania company to fill a hole.

crufty, cruftier

Geek-speak for something that's poorly built or overly complex. Often used to describe new software features that are added at the expense of functionality. "The latest upgrade from Microsoft is **cruftier**." Possibly named for Cruft Hall at Harvard, the physics building, which would have had a lot of hackers passing through it over the years.

cryptonoia
The paranoid tendency to read meaning into things that aren't there. "**Cryptonoiacs** can't read the back of a cereal box without finding a hidden conspiracy."

cube farm
What most workplaces have become. It's a large open space within an office that's been subdivided into endless rows of cubicles.

cubicle vultures
Office mates who circle a laid-off worker's desk and swoop in to pick it clean — appropriating prized chairs, lamps, file cabinets, staplers, etc., for their own cubicles.

cup-holder cuisine
Food packaged to fit in the cup holder of a car and marketed to commuters who feel compelled to eat while driving — and who, of course, are using their free hand to hold their cell phone.

customer experience team

The modern company has become obsessed in controlling the "customer experience" in relation to its products. As a result, **Customer Experience Teams** are springing up everywhere. In some cases, they replace the old **Customer Service Team**. In any event, their job is to make sure the customer has a "positive" experience when interacting with the company or its products.

customer facing

Not a sewing term. In the software world, it's what the customer sees and interacts with — frequently the image presented on a computer screen. In business, **customer facing** is what customers encounter when they interact with a company, such as sales or customer service people.

customer intimacy

Corporate attempt to "get close to the customer" that basically invades buyers' privacy by monitoring (and databasing) their purchases, inquiries, requests, etc., in order to personalize products and services — therefore boosting sales and customer loyalty.

customer relationship management

A fancy term that means you should treat customers as individuals and customize what you do to make them happy. Large companies do this with multimillion-dollar computer systems. Small companies generally do it with a handshake and a smile.

customer-centric

This comes from the process of taking any noun and tacking "centric" to the end of it. In this case, it means a business, product or service is focused or "centered" on the customer. "Our new product line was produced using a **customer-centric** process." Now there's a novel concept.

C-wall

An academic requirement where a student must receive at least a C grade in a prerequisite course in order to register for a more advanced course. Failure to breach the **C-wall** often results in a change in major, change in career plans or change in schools.

cyberbalkanization

Online narrow-mindedness. A product of the Internet's ability to bring together narrowly-focused, like-minded individuals who increasingly know and care more and more about less and less.

cyberbeggars

Individuals who create their own Web sites in order to beg for cash to pay off their debts and actually get people to send them money. Also known as *e-panhandling*. Note of caution: Beware **cyberbeggars** who accept credit cards. *See **bleggars***

cyberbullying
To bully or badger someone electronically, via email, text messaging, IMing, etc.

cyberchondriacs
People who obsessively pore through health Web sites in search of diseases and symptoms with which to misdiagnose themselves.

cyberskeptics
A growing group of legal experts who think the need for separate "cyberlaws" to govern the "cybercitizens" of "cyberspace" is "cybersilly." They argue that something that happens online should be treated the same way it is treated if it occurs on Main Street.

cyberslackers
Employees who use the company Internet connection during work hours to surf the Net, shop, play games, check stock prices, etc.

cycles
We used to have life cycles and economic cycles, but more and more it's a cool way of referring to how much time you have available. "I don't have the **cycles** to attend that meeting today." Or: "Give it to Jackson, he has the **cycles**."

data cholesterol

The build-up of information or traffic that slows down a software application's ability to perform. "Outerbay's technology improves performance of mission-critical Oracle applications up to 40% by eliminating the **data cholesterol** that builds with transaction volume."

data dump

Basically, it's a debriefing. A person working on a project does a **data dump** for the person taking over the project. It also refers to a brainstorming session where everyone contributes ideas. Another name for this is *brain dump*.

data mart

Using a **data mart** means you're too cheap to spend the money to buy a big enough computer system to handle all of your business needs. Instead of putting all of your business information in one system (a data warehouse), you continue to use several different computer systems to run your business (one for accounting, one for customer service, another for sales, etc.).

data point

Once a hard number that could be graphed, it's now become any anecdote or opinion disguised as fact that can be used to persuade others. "I think we need a few more data points before we can make that decision." Also, a bullet point in a PowerPoint presentation.

data shadow
The trail of digital information you leave behind every time you use a credit card, send an email, browse the Web or use a cell phone.

data smog
Too much information. A Google search that turns up six million references would be data smog.

dataveillance
Tracking an individual by following the data trail left each time he or she uses a credit card, cell phone or the Internet. See *data shadow*

Day 2 project
Anything that's not on the immediate horizon or is a low priority. "Don't worry about that now, that's a **Day 2 project**." Loosely translated: "That's a nice idea, but don't hold your breath."

DBT
Death by Tweakage. When a product or project fails due to unnecessary tinkering or too many last-minute revisions. "Why did the new product fail?" "It had the **DBTs**."

dead peasants insurance

A corporate "win-win" bet on your life. The practice of companies taking out life insurance policies on their own employees (often without them knowing it) while designating the company as beneficiary. If the employee dies young, the company gets tax-free death benefits. If the employee lives long, it has a long-running tax break. Also known as *janitors' insurance*.

deck

A staple of every modern business meeting – another name for the PowerPoint "slide" show. "There were only 12 slides in the **deck**, but the presentation lasted an hour."

deconflicted

Military-speak for the elimination of conflicts. This can be done several ways. One is to identify and synchronize your planes, troops, etc., so their missions do not conflict. Another is to control a given area by the elimination of an opposing force. "The skies above Iraq have been **deconflicted**." And, of course, you hear it in business now. "The software allows you to filter and sort work groups to create **deconflicted** schedules."

deep dive

To explore an issue or subject in-depth. "We did a **deep dive** on that market. There's just nothing there."

deep-domain expertise

A favorite of consultants, particularly in the technical arena. It simply means they have expertise in a particular area. The term "deep domain" is for extra emphasis. In other words: "We know what we're talking about when it comes to this particular subject; in fact, we really, really know what we're talking about."

deer market

Neither a bear market nor a bull market. It's when the market is flat and not moving in either direction. Investors are indecisive - like deer frozen in the headlights.

defenestrate

The original usage, dating from the 17th century, meant "to execute by throwing someone out a window." In today's geek-speak, it means to stop using Microsoft Windows. "The users are much happier since we chose to **defenestrate** the servers and workstations at this location."

deferred success

Term proposed by a group of British educators to replace the word "failed" to avoid demoralizing students.

defrag

Once we just "defragged" our hard drives, now we're "defragging" our brains. "I'm too tired to go out tonight. I want to stay home, have a quiet drink and **defrag**." Rest, relax and mentally recharge.

Diplomatically said

*Real diplo-babble from a
White House briefing:*

There was a discussion of bilateral issues yesterday and some multilateral issues involving nonproliferation, some areas where, I think, we've done quite a bit of good work — on areas related to CTBT and the Chemical Weapons Convention — but also some of our concerns about nonproliferation. We've got a continuing dialogue at the expert level on there and we're going to have a continuing series of discussions on that. We believe that we've made significant progress over the last several months on that issue, but we've got a good deal more work to go.

deja moo
The nagging feeling that you've heard this bull before.

deja poo
The feeling that you've stepped in this bull before.

deliverable
A perfectly legitimate word that has been reduced to consultant-speak. It generally means work promised to be completed by a certain time. "This project has 14 **deliverables**."

demand-side management
Leveling out the peaks and valleys of demand for a company's product. For example, electric utilities regularly offer incentives to companies that shift their power usage from peak times to off-peak times. See *congestion pricing*

denial-of-service attack
Any attempt to prevent legitimate users from accessing your Web site or sending you email, usually accomplished by flooding your servers with page requests or thousands of email messages. This requires slightly above average technical skill and a malicious mindset.

de-risk
Corporate-speak for reducing risk. "We continue to **de-risk** our revenue profile with stronger growth in Europe."

desktime
Those brief periods between meetings when you're actually sitting at your desk working. "I'll need a little **desktime** between the offsite strategy meeting and the afternoon brainstorming session so I can schedule tomorrow's team status meeting."

destinesia
A temporary condition that explains the dumb blank look on your face when you arrive at your destination but can't remember why you're there. *See **synlapse***

dial it back
To tone it down or take a step back. As in turn the dial back a notch. "Your press release is pushing believability. **Dial it back**."

dialogue
Apparently no one talks during business meetings any more. Instead, everyone **dialogues**. "Let's **dialogue** about the new product launch."

digital amnesia

The result of being so overwhelmed by the availability, speed and volume of digital information that you can't remember any of it (or where you might have put it on your hard drive).

dot crash

The Internet has been great for buzzword creation, so it's logical that the crash of the Internet economy created its own collection. **Dot carnage** was the aftermath of the collapse, aptly describing the digital landscape littered with broken dreams and hordes of people looking for work. This message was spotted on a listserv: "My company may become another victim of the **dot carnage** because my paycheck is now delayed by 'a few days'." Other dot.com crash buzzwords include **dot.bomb** (the crash itself) and **dot.calm** (the calm period after the crash).

digital denial

The failure of a company or industry to accept that the Internet has changed the world and made their business model obsolete. Example: The recording industry, desperate to maintain the status quo, has turned to suing its own customers.

digital dieting

Thanks to digital photography and PhotoShop, more and more folks are losing weight by removing pixels, not pounds. Wrinkles and gray hair are disappearing, too.

Digital Divide

More imposing than the Continental Divide. It's the disturbing gap between the Haves and Have Nots of society. The Haves are able to keep abreast of the changes caused by technological advances. The Have Nots are getting further behind because they can't afford computers, Internet access, etc. This is clearly being seen in the education system, where poorly funded schools are producing graduates who are not prepared for the digital world they're stepping into.

digiteria

Geek-speak for a coffee shop, restaurant, bar or other public place where "cool people" meet in a Wi-Fi environment.

DINOs

Democrats in Name Only. Despite their party affiliation, they sound and act like Republicans. Their counterparts across the aisle: RINOs.

diplo-speak, diplo-babble

Diplo-speak is a coded language spoken by diplomats to "send a message" without actually committing to anything. **Diplo-babble**, on the other hand, is laden with fuzzy buzzwords and contains no message at all. *See sidebar on next page*

directionally correct

Consultant-speak for "Trust us. We don't have a specific answer, but if you go in this general direction we think you'll be making the right decision."

Director of First Impressions

A receptionist. Once the punch line of an Internet joke, it's now an actual job title at some companies.

disambiguate

To remove ambiguities. To make clear. Used extensively by software developers, as in: "Before we go gold, we need to **disambiguate** the help menu verbiage."

disclude

Growing in use, particularly among the computer crowd and marketers, it simply means "to not include." "We **disclude** those who don't have a net worth of at least $1 million."

dispense suspense

Those milliseconds between making a vending machine selection and it successfully dropping down for you to retrieve — during which you silently scream to the bag of chips, "Don't get stuck, DON'T GET STUCK!"

Dixie-Chicked

To be reviled or boycotted for voicing an unpopular political sentiment. "Dreamworks is worried that Chris Rock may criticize Bush and the movie will get **Dixie-Chicked**." Refers to the band Dixie Chicks, which was criticized after the lead singer said she was embarrassed for Texas because of George Bush.

Dixie Cup

A small economy car. After being involved in an accident, it is discarded like a used Dixie Cup.

DKTM

An abbreviation often added to an email when the writer wants the recipient to know that he doesn't support or agree with the proposal he has been elected to deliver. Stands for: Don't Kill The Messenger.

DNA trip

The annoying act of pushing one's beliefs, ethnic heritage or traditions on others. "Jack's on a real **DNA trip**."

document polish

Fancy phrases and buzzwords added to reports or other documents that sound important or impressive — but add nothing meaningful to the content.

docusoap

A term that appears to more accurately describe the genre known as "Reality TV." Half documentary, half soap opera.

dog-whistle politics

A political message that works much like a high-pitched dog-whistle. It's inaudible or ignored by most of us, but is heard clearly by the target audience.

dooced

To get fired for something you wrote in your personal blog. Named after Heather Armstrong's Web site dooce.com. Heather was one of the first to get sacked for her musings.

dopeler effect

The tendency of stupid ideas to seem smarter when they come at you rapidly.

dormandise

To resurrect dormant brand names to take advantage of ad campaigns that are still rattling around in the collective consumer conscience — even though the products themselves may have long ceased to exist. Because of **dormandisation** we can once again read Life Magazine while drinking Ovaltine in our VW Beetles.

dot.con, dot-con

An Internet scam.

dot-conomy

Do we really need to explain this? It is just one in the continuous line of language bastardizations having to do with the Internet. It's what happens when a BuzzMaker runs into a word he can't just add the letter e to.

dot-corps

Corporations that primarily exist on the Internet. They have few — if any — physical assets. Most died in April 2000 when the stock market took its pound of flesh.

dotted line

Organizational-speak for employees who do not have direct reporting responsibility to a manager, but share account or customer responsibilities. Refers to the dotted lines in organizational charts that indicate an indirect relationship between an employee and a manager. "Bob reports to the sales team, but has a **dotted line** to Jane, who manages customer service."

double drunk

Police-speak for someone whose blood alcohol level registers twice the legal limit on the Breathalyzer.

double-click

To give more attention to or evaluate in depth. Derived from double-clicking on a file to open it. "Let's start with the historical data, and after that we can **double-click** on the pro formas."

downline

A term in multi-level marketing (MLM) that describes the people who work beneath you (down the line). Your job is to recruit them to sell your products. In return, you get a percentage of their sales. Their job is to recruit people below them. In return, they get a percentage of their recruits' sales. And so do you. It spirals down and down.

drailing

Pounding out email messages (which you'll probably regret) to your friends, bosses, co-workers, etc., while drunk.

DRIB

Don't Read If Busy. An acronym used in subject lines by thoughtful and courteous email senders, which pretty much guarantees an email will never be opened and read.

drill down

In the early days of the Web, it was the process of clicking on hyperlinks to go deeper and deeper into a Web site to find increasingly minute detail. Now a good Web site gives you everything you need in one or two clicks. So NOW the term applies to other parts of business. As a verb, it means to investigate something thoroughly; to discuss in detail. "We need to get together and really **drill down** on this." As a noun, it's the result of that process: "Do you have the **drill down** on that report for me?"

drink the Kool-Aid

This truly tasteless buzz phrase has its roots in the Jim Jones' cult that committed suicide in Guyana in 1978. The cyanide-laced concoction they drank was made from a powdered fruit drink. For the record, it was NOT Kool-Aid. Now, back to the definition: It means that one wholly buys into a philosophy. "Even though the company had zero chance of succeeding, we were all naive enough to **drink the Kool-Aid**." Of course, Jim Jones didn't offer stock options.

drinking from a fire hose

Overwhelmed. Taking on too much of a workload.

drip irrigation

In marketing, it's the process of slowly building a customer file. Never ask them for too much of their private information at one time. Get a little bit here, a little bit there, until you have what you need. It supposedly is the best way to build a relationship with the customer. Comes from the agricultural process of slowly watering crops to avoid drowning them.

drip marketing

Marketers love to steal terms from the agricultural world, but this one's not all wet. **Drip marketing** is the process of slowly convincing prospects to buy your products by dribbling different pieces of marketing — postcards, flyers, email, ads — over a long period of time.

drive-by download

A software program that automatically downloads to your computer — often without your consent or knowledge and for nefarious purposes.

drive-by VCs

Venture Capitalists who put money into a company and then abandon it at the first sign of trouble. They were easy to spot in April 2000, when Internet stocks plunged and they fled the scene of the crime.

druce, druced

To go to extraordinary lengths to avoid consequences for one's actions. To shamelessly manipulate the courts to skirt justice. "He **druced** the IRS by shredding the paperwork and blaming it on his partner." Coined in honor of former Pennsylvania state legislator Thomas Druce, who has spent years trying to duck responsibility for killing a man in a hit-and-run accident.

drunch

A combination lunch and dinner. It often starts out as a late lunch, but then runs into the dinner hour (or later). **Drunches** are generally fueled with an abundance of liquid libations.

Dub-dub-dub

Short for w-w-w. You'll often hear techies say this when giving another techie a URL. "Hey, can you check out this site? Go to **dub-dub-dub**.buzzwhack.com."

duck shuffler

Just when you get all your "ducks in a row," a **duck shuffler** — usually someone in upper management — comes around and rearranges them for you.

duppie

A depressed urban professional. **Duppies** are often overeducated and underemployed — working menial jobs until the job market improves.

E2E

Eyeball-to-eyeball. For those who want something more specific than F2F (face-to-face) contact with a customer or employee.

EADD

Entrepreneurial Attention Deficit Disorder. A common condition among entrepreneurial business executives. They start up one company, get bored and leave to start up another company.

eagle system

To search by circling or hovering above a fixed object until spying the desired target. "I type using the **eagle system**."

early birding

A marketing strategy that creates enough buzz to convince consumers to pre-purchase a new product not to get a discount, but to be among the first to own it.

EBBS

Given how companies obfuscate earning reports in an attempt to put the best possible spin on them, it's nearly impossible to figure out real performance. So David Blitzer, chief investment strategist for Standard & Poor's Corp., coined **EBBS**: Earnings Before Bad Stuff.

e-cubator
The business world has long had "incubators" where ideas are hatched and nurtured into companies. The BuzzMakers, of course, felt anything to do with the Internet had to be different and cutting edge. Therefore, incubators that specialize in Internet startups or e-business ideas are called **e-cubators**.

e-dress or edress
A buzz term created by those who feel "email address" is simply too mundane.

edu-marketing
The use of free educational content to generate sales leads. All those Web sites offering free white papers, special reports, exclusive studies, etc., are further proof that there is no such thing as a free lunch. In return for their free educational material, expect to give up your name and email address, if not more.

e-dundant
The tendency of middle managers to follow up a subordinate's email with one of their own to add unnecessary emphasis or make it look like it the idea was originally their own.

effectivity
The length of time something is valid or "effective." Computer programming term that describes the validity of data, but now used by other departments, such as marketing, in reference to just about everything.

efforting
Another example of "verbing." "We're **efforting** a follow-up on the president's report."

ego surfing
Searching the Web to see how many times your name turns up and what others are saying about you. "The report is late because Jack spent the morning **ego surfing**." See **narcissurfing**

electronify
The process of turning paper-based data into electronic or digital form. See **webify**

eload
The quantity of email a person receives. "We're trying to reduce our staff's **eload**."

email ellipsia
The mind-numbing use of ellipses ... instead of proper punctuation ... in email ... then again ... most email messages are little more than a series of sentence fragments ... and random thoughts ... so maybe it's not abuse.

email train
An email message that grows in length as people reply without deleting the previous responses.

embullishment
What almost all embellishment really is.

emerging technology
A reference to any technology that's being developed. If you're really lucky it's in beta testing. More than likely it's just a promise of future development and is frequently just a gleam in someone's eye.

employee rustout
A workplace malady in which an employee's potential is underused and his/her performance is mediocre. Rustout is more subtle and insidious than its better known counterpart, employee burnout.

employee surfboarding
When supervisors ride (and take credit for) the wave of success created by the hard work and ideas of their best employees.

empowerment with fences
The concept of empowering workers to make decisions on their own as long as they don't stray beyond the boundaries set by the company.

empty suit

An executive in upper management who lacks the knowledge, experience, skills and/or intellect to hold the position. "The director of marketing is an **empty suit**." Female **empty suits** are also known as a "hollow bunnies" (from hollow chocolate Easter bunnies).

EMV

EMail Voice. The tone of a person's voice on the phone that signals he's reading his email instead of listening to you. See **IMpause** and **surfer's voice**

engagement synopsis

The latest in consultant-ese. An "engagement" is the work a consultant does for a client. "Synopsis" is an outline of that work. Together they're simply a summary of a case study used to promote the consultant's business.

Enron

To undermine the future. A product of the Enron scandal, this new verb comes courtesy of former Sen. Tom Daschle. "I don't want to **Enron** the American people. I don't want to see them holding the bag at the end of the day just like Enron employees have held the bag."

Enronym

Any word formed from the base "Enron," usually signifying some form of corporate malfeasance. Recently spotted **Enronyms**: Enronitis, Enronify, Enronomics.

e-pending
The attempt by marketers to match an email address to your real-world info in order to "more effectively" market to you.

escape ring
A planned call or beep from a co-worker that allows you to feign an emergency in order to escape a particularly boring or meaningless meeting.

e-ternative
An alternative with an electronic bent. Email is an **e-ternative** to snail-mail.

etherface
The impersonal discourse with another person via email or other Internet-based communication.

eThrombosis
Coined by medical researchers who believe that sitting too long in front of a computer can cause deep vein thrombosis. To prevent life-threatening blood clots from forming, they recommend that computer users stand up every couple of hours and walk around. Getting a real life wouldn't hurt either.

event horizon
A point in your life, business, career, etc., when something big is going to happen and your life will be

significantly changed. Once known as a "turning point." For Baby Boomers, it's called a mid-life crisis.

evergreening
The process of regularly updating or upgrading something to keep it "fresh" or current. Schools have plans for **evergreening** their computers. Web sites are **evergreening** content. Pharmaceutical companies are **evergreening** drug patents.

Evernet
Thanks to PCs, pagers, TV, digital phones, etc., you can be continuously connected to the Internet — redubbed the **Evernet**. Apparently coined by Thomas Friedman, author and New York Times correspondent.

exceedance
A term created by those who like to measure things and treasured by government bureaucrats. It's a common term in the world of pollutants. Simply, it's the amount by which something exceeds a standard or permissible measurement. "An ozone **exceedance** occurs when ozone levels recorded at any of the regional monitoring sites reach 125 parts per billion or greater."

extraview
A second round interview with an applicant you feel obligated to meet again, even though another candidate already has won the job.

eye chart

An information-laden PowerPoint slide with small type. Often introduced with: "I know this slide is tough to see, but..." Example: "As we showed on the bottom line of the **eye chart** I covered a few minutes ago, we had a 31% increase in net revenue."

F2F

With email, webinars and teleconferencing on the rise, it was only a matter of time before we needed an abbreviated way to make "face-to-face" meetings sound unique.

fabless

Techie-speak for a semiconductor company that designs and markets computer chips, but outsources the manufacturing. A "fab" company, on the other hand, has the facilities to "fabricate" its own chips.

face guy

A chief executive hired primarily because he looks like an "executive" and sounds good on TV.

face time

Ambitious workers used to fight for **face time** with the boss. Salespeople wanted more **face time** with customers. In these days of telecommuting, it takes on an expanded meaning. It's the time that telecommuters physically meet the co-workers they normally interact with through email, chat or video-conferencing. "I'll be in the office Thursday so we can do a little **face time**."

fact witness
Someone who actually has direct knowledge of an event. The opposite of an "expert witness," who simply renders opinions based on expertise.

fact-based management
A novel concept touted by business gurus for improving profits. First, evaluate and measure a given business process, then use those "facts" to streamline it.

failing in
When your grades aren't bad enough to flunk out, but they're so poor you can't transfer enough credits to another university to make it worthwhile. So you plug along with a 1.8 GPA.

faith-based intelligence
A top-down approach to management in which the top executives' philosophy is: "We know the answers — now give us the intelligence to support those answers."

fat-fingered
To hit the wrong button, key, etc., when dialing, typing, etc. While we like to blame it on poorly designed keyboards and keypads, most of the time it's because we're simply klutzes. "Here's the correct URL. I **fat-fingered** it the first time."

faulty-tasking
When multi-tasking goes awry.

FEMA approach

When a problem arises, meetings are held and action plans drawn up, but no one does anything. Refers to the Federal Emergency Management Agency's stellar response to Hurricane Katrina.

filther

Any system used to filter out email filth or block access to pornographic Web sites.

financial pit stop

To refuel one's financial resources. For the self-employed, it's taking a meaningless (but paying) job to survive until the economy regains its health or the next venture comes along.

first eyes

The first Web page you look at after you sign on gets **first eyes**. The term is used a lot by ISPs (Internet Service Providers) and portals. Basically, it refers to getting the first crack at selling/influencing a Web user.

first mover

In business, it's the company that gets its new innovative product, service, or solution to market first. Supposedly, this gives them a "**first-mover** advantage" and the opportunity to dominate the market. Amazon.com was considered to have the "**first-mover** advantage." But marketing research shows that being first doesn't guarantee long-term success. There are plenty of tortoises that started slowly but won the day.

Fisher-Priced

Having toy-like qualities. Often used by techies to describe less than desirable hardware or software. "Bob, have you tested Windows XP?" "Yeah Dan, it's completely **Fisher-Priced**."

fisk, fisked

To stretch or distort the truth for your own purposes. Coined by bloggers to describe British journalist Robert Fisk's columns and reports. Someone who has been **fisked** has had his or her views, actions, etc., misrepresented.

five nines

Techie-speak for a system that can stay up 99.999% of the time. Considered the highest number realistically achievable. "We're going to need **five nines** from this system."

flag conservatives

"Conservative" politicians who pay only lip service to conservative values. They wrap themselves in the flag and toss around words like "evil" in order to keep from narrowing their political base. See **DINOs**

flange-up

To match up. In plumbing and oil drilling, it's about connecting pipes. In the rest of the business world, when two ideas, projects or companies work well together they **flange-up**.

Flashturbation

The superfluous use of Macromedia Flash animation on a Web site that adds little or no value. The result of a Web design team "pleasuring" itself.

flies

People who are sucked into the Web by clever marketing strategies that offer free points, coupons and credit toward merchandise. They spend hours glued to their computers viewing ads so they can rack up the "rewards."

flu day

Much like snow days, schools are now taking **flu days**. To prevent or reduce the spread of the flu, schools and school districts will shut down until the illness subsides.

fly the wrong flag

Behaving or acting in a manner deemed inappropriate by corporate culture. Example: A GM executive driving a Ford Explorer.

flyblogged

The result of unwanted spam being posted to an open blog, just as flies stick to flypaper. "I have just been comprehensively **flyblogged**." Coined by technology analyst Bill Thompson.

FOBIO

Frequently Outwitted By Inanimate Objects. A condition commonly associated with the assembly of do-it-yourself furniture or toys with lots of parts. Peak period generally occurs on Christmas Eve.

follicularly disenfranchised

To be bald.

forklift upgrade

For some reason, the tech world loves to use industrial terms to explain things. A **forklift upgrade** is a massive overhaul of a computer network or system, which will require a major investment of hardware.

form factor

In computer-speak, it refers to the size, shape or physical arrangement of computer hardware. "If you're looking for a really cool **form factor**, you might try the Tablet PC."

forward-worthy

Email (often of a humorous nature) deemed worthy of being passed along to friends and colleagues. Term is generally used by folks who claim they "rarely" or "never" forward such stuff. "I found this Buzzword of the Day **forward-worthy**. Hope you like it."

freemium

Business model where you give your basic services away for free, but then charge a premium for advanced or extra features.

frendor

A vendor who is preferred over others in the market, perhaps because the salesperson regularly plays golf with the boss.

fritterware

Software that entices users to spend time tweaking their work with little or no gain in productivity. Also used to describe just about any computer game played during work hours when the boss isn't looking.

frying spam

The increasingly time-consuming morning ritual of deleting spam from your inbox.

FUD Factor

When a company wants to play with the customer's head, it implements the **FUD Factor**: Fear, Uncertainty and Doubt. Example: If Company A launches a new product, Company Z will spin the **FUD Factor** about A's product. The goal is to delay any buying decision until Company Z can create its own version of the product.

furkid
A pampered pet that's treated like more like a child than a pet.

future-proof
To design or build a product or system that won't be made obsolete by the next wave of technological advancements. Of course, very few things are truly **future-proof**, although the paper clip has proven to be amazingly close.

Say what?

Excerpt from a real press release:

The addition of Murgator software and Nanu Systems services to the TYP Select Program will help TYP customers optimize their business continuance planning efforts with their business and IT stakeholders. Murgator users can easily develop business impact analysis, as well as create, manage, and distribute business continuity and recovery plans across the organization. Murgator also allows organizations to automate the change management process of maintaining business continuance plans.

gathering string

The act of collecting seemingly unconnected facts, figures and data that eventually support a thesis. "Right now, I'm just **gathering string**. We'll see where it takes us later."

gatored

You've been gatored when you're visiting one Web site and find yourself being hijacked and whisked to a competitor's site. Named for a plug-in from Gator.com that does the dirty work. Also known as *hijackware*.

geek chic

Styles or fashions favored by computer geeks. (Once upon a time no one thought geeks had either.)

geek handshake

The process of introducing yourself to someone by text messaging your business card info, even though he or she may only be 10 feet away.

Generation C

Describes the growing group of consumers who are obsessed with generating their own "content" — expressing creative urges by snapping photos with camera phones, producing movies on home computers for general distribution, or running personal blogs. Of course, just because the masses can do it doesn't make it "art."

Generation D

Unlike Generations X and Y, **Generation D**(igital) is not determined by age. It's the group of people who are completely at ease with the digital revolution, whether they're 8 or 80.

Generation O

Move aside Gen Xers! The O stands for obesity, since the latest generation of kids are the fattest in history.

Generica

What the American landscape has become. One continuous blend of fast food joints, strip malls and subdivisions.

ghost work

Following a layoff, it's the workload absorbed by the surviving staff — generally with little notice or proper training.

Giuliani-esque

Grace and strength under pressure. A term coined by former CBS anchor Dan Rather after watching the extraordinary performance of New York Mayor Rudolph Giuliani in the aftermath of the Sept. 11 terrorist attacks.

Global 3500

A term bandied about as if it were an official organization. "We're a **Global 3500** company." Defined by Forrester Research as the largest 3,500 companies in the world. Formerly the Global 2000.

global responsibilities

Once upon a time it meant you had responsibility for operations, projects or people scattered around the world. Now every team leader has **global responsibilities** — even when his staff of three people sit next to one another in the same room.

globesity

Worldwide obesity. While Americans are still kings of obesity, we've exported enough junk food that the rest of the world appears to be catching up.

glocalize

It's the "positive" side of globalization. The ability of a culture or country to absorb enriching influences of other cultures without being overwhelmed. Apparently coined by author Thomas Friedman.

godcasting

Any regular religious or inspirational podcast. **Godcasts** are among the highest-ranking podcasts. The Catholic Insider program regularly ranks in the top 20 on PodcastAlley.com.

going forward
An executive's way of saying "in the future." "We lost $10 million last quarter, but **going forward** we'll execute our vision more proactively." Do companies ever "go backward"?

golden bungee
A lucrative executive severance package that not only pays the executive to step down from his or her current position, but includes a new employment contract with lucrative pay to continue with the company in another role.

Goldilocks Economy
When the economy isn't too hot to cause inflation or too cold to cause a recession. It's just right.

golfmail
The result of forwarding your office phone, email, etc., to your wireless phone, allowing you to play 18 holes while maintaining the illusion for customers (and the boss) that you're at your desk.

Googlejuice
What your Web site has if appears naturally near the top of a Google search (without having to pay for it). "BuzzWhack.com has Googlejuice!"

GOLFMAIL

Google politics

To make a thousand accusations — none of which are substantiated.

Google share

The amount of real estate one gets on the first page of a Google search. "If we name our site 'Harvest,' we won't get enough **Google share**."

Google stalk

The act of using Google to research a potential boyfriend or girlfriend with the hope of obtaining information as to his or her interests.

Googlephobia

The fear that Google is taking over everything and threatening to become the next Microsoft.

Googleplexity

When a project appears to be simple, but becomes more complex after closer examination — requiring enormous resources, time and patience to complete. "The new accounting system looked so easy, but it's taken us a month to get running. It's a **Googleplexity**." Derived from the fact that the search engine Google appears to be very simple, but uses complicated, sophisticated algorithms behind the scenes.

Googleproof

One of the few benefits of sharing a name with a celebrity. It's virtually impossible for anyone to "Google" or find out about you using an Internet search engine. You're **Googleproof**.

Googleverse

Another sign that Google is dominating our world. It's the collection of Web pages, images or content indexed or otherwise connected to Google and therefore now part of the Google universe.

Googlewash

An effort by bloggers to change the meaning of a new word, term or phrase by peppering their Web logs with an alternate meaning. Result: A search using Google will turn up thousands of pages with the altered definition, while the pages carrying the original and intended usage get buried.

Googlewhack

The result of Googlewhacking, a game invented by search-obsessed fans of Google.com. Object: Type two words into the Google search line with the hope of getting a single search result. If you see "Results 1-1 of 1," you're a winner (and clearly have too much time on your hands).

granularity, granular

Sand and sugar are granular. But when business execs get down to the nitty-gritty, they're dealing in the **granularity**. It's the finite details or specific fine points of a proposal or deal.

greenwash

The process of touting the environmental benefits of a product or policy in order to deflect attention from other less savory aspects.

grid rage

The total frustration that comes from being unable to complete the New York Times Saturday (or Sunday) crossword puzzle.

gridmaster

To plan in obsessive detail and assign a moment-by-moment timeline for a project's development. "James **gridmastered** the software project right up to its release date."

gription

Traction.

Groundhog Day

When a company's management ignores obvious problems, allowing them to resurface on a daily basis. Named for the Bill Murray movie of the same name, in which Murray's character keeps waking up on Groundhog Day over and over.

group think

A group dynamic that discourages critical thinking in the decision-making process and encourages conformity to existing beliefs. "The congressional report accused the CIA of **group think** in its analysis of pre-Iraq War intelligence."

Integrated proactive solutions

Excerpt from a real press release:

RQI enables organizations to proactively manage their customers, employees, dealers and franchisees using real time business intelligence solutions through an integrated portfolio. RQI provides clients the insights to make real-time strategic and tactical decisions that impact Brand Performance.

hacktivist

Someone who combines hacking skills with activism to attack, shut down or deface target Web sites as a form of political protest. It's a form of electronic civil disobedience. They're experts of the "virtual sit-in."

hairball

Any tangled mess. Often refers to poorly written computer code — with Microsoft's name frequently invoked — but could simply be any organization's maze of rules and regulations.

ham

Legitimate email messages that get filtered or block-deleted in your attempt to separate the "real meat" from the spam.

hamsterize

To use manual labor in lieu of technology. Instead of spending money on technology, a company will employ a bunch of $8-an-hour "hamsters" to do the job.

handraulics

A manual process. "We loaded the software **handraulically** — we did it by hand."

hang-time
When your computer freezes and you can't do anything. "I've got some **hang-time**, so I'll balance the checkbook."

heat-seeking workforce
A product of the dot-com boom. It's workers who flock to the hot companies, then move on whenever the stock price drops.

heavy lifting
The hard work. As in: "The design team did the **heavy lifting**, we just marketed and sold the product."

hedonic treadmill
As your income rises, your expectations and desires rise in concert. Problem: There's seldom a matching increase in happiness or satisfaction. In other words, the more you get, the more you want and the less you enjoy it.

helicopter mom
An overprotective and overly-involved mom. **Helicopter moms** can't simply drop their kids off at school. They must visit their children's classroom daily to hover and see how they are doing — embarrassing the child and irritating the teacher.

helicopter view
A synonym for overview. "Let's get together and take a **helicopter view** of the situation." See *10,000-foot view*

HEAT-SEEKING WORKFORCE

herding cats

Any frustrating or near impossible task. "Jeez, trying to get corporate approval is like **herding cats**."

hijackware

Any software or plug-in that whisks you from the Web site you're perusing to a competitor's site. Also known as *scumware*. See **gatored**

himbo

A male bimbo.

HiPo list

A group of generally younger employees thought to have High Potential (HiPo) and possessing the right stuff to become future corporate execs — after appropriate brainwashing, er, training, of course.

hip-pop

Hip-hop that's become so commercialized it appeals more to suburban mallrats than urban youth. Puff Daddy may have started out as hip-hop, but P. Diddy (now Diddy) is pure **hip-pop**.

hiptop

A multifunction wireless device that's part cell phone, camera, game console, Internet browser, PDA, etc., which is spawning its own blogs, web portals and a culture known as the **Hiptop** Nation.

homeshoring

The growing practice of having call center or customer service reps work from their homes. Also called *homesourcing*. There are more than 100,000 such employees in the U.S. alone.

homing from work

While some people are working from home, most of us are using the latest technology for **homing from work** — keeping in touch with our kids using cell phones, text messages, virtual networks, etc. Once frowned upon as doing "personal business on company time," it's now encouraged at some companies so employees don't feel guilty about working late. Of course, some of us are simply tapping into our home computers so we can update our resumes.

hoovering

The fine of art of sucking up. (Note: **Hoovering**, adapted from the name of a vacuum cleaner, has numerous definitions — including a few dirty ones. This just happens to be our favorite.)

horked

Broken, confused or trashed. Generally describes software or hardware that no longer works.

hot desking
When workers have no permanent workstation or desk and are assigned temporary workspace based on current need. The "official" corporate term is "location independent working." Among workers it's known as being homeless.

hotsquatting
Tapping (often illegally) into open Wi-Fi connections.

Cop talk?

*Do police officers really talk like this?
Only in press releases:*

Police Director Anthony Smith called the driving simulator, "An extremely beneficial and potentially life-saving training tool that provides a realistic training field in a risk-free environment. Our officers routinely travel through dense traffic en route to emergencies and this proactive training measure should reduce the risk of accidents and injuries."

human gateway

An annoying person who constantly posts "news" from one email discussion list to another, whether it's relevant or not.

hydraulics of the situation

An MBA buzzword meaning to understand how something works in order to make the necessary adjustments.

hypertasking

While we're frequently forced to multitask just to keep up at work, **hypertasking** is a choice for those who thrive on doing more than one thing at a time. A **hypertasker** combines many tasks into one in order to experience more. He may exercise, play tourist and conduct business at the same time by riding his bike through the Blue Ridge Mountains while running a business meeting via his wireless headset.

IAMS

It's About Me Stupid. An attitude taken by employees that makes them feel justified doing personal things on company time. "I'm not finishing that project today. I haven't had sufficient **IAMS** time."

ID-10T error

IT code word for user error. **ID-10T** translates to "idiot."

I-mail

Email sent to peers, subordinates, supervisors, etc., that excessively uses the pronoun "I." Such messages usually extol the achievements of the sender for completing a given task — even if it's just a routine assignment.

immi-merce

Thanks to the Internet, immigrants are increasingly transferring their cash back home by shopping at Web sites based in their native countries.

impactful, impactfulness

Two contrived words created by folks who obviously felt the word "impact" needed a little extra "oomph." Examples: "The two companies are forging an **impactful** strategic alliance." "Entries will be judged on their overall effectiveness and creative **impactfulness**."

IMpause

The annoying silence on the other end of the phone as the person you're talking to pauses to answer an Instant Message.

in silico

The computer version of "in vitro." "We've created a computer model of the forest fire and now we're letting it burn **in silico** to see what it might do."

inch pebbles

Small, incremental achievements. Imagine what you'd get if you smashed a milestone — a lot of **inch pebbles**.

Individual Contributor (IC)

Consultant-speak used to distinguish the peons who do all the work from the folks in management roles. "The project failed due to low **IC** morale."

infonesia, Internesia

Infonesia is the inability to remember where you spotted a piece of information (newspaper, email, TV, etc.). **Internesia** is when you can't remember which Web site the info came from or which bookmark might get you back there.

information architect

A hugely inventive and successful way in which librarians (and a host of other wannabes) have made themselves relevant to computers and the Internet. An **information architect's** job is to balance the needs of Web site sponsors, users and designers so that information is presented in a manner that makes all concerned happier — and the architect richer.

information leakage

Digital equivalent of "loose lips sink ships."
Information leakage results when a programming flaw inadvertently reveals sensitive information as data passes through the Internet. Result: Someone spotting the flaw could use that info to hack the originating computer system.

information touchpoint

Any contact in which information is shared or transferred. Yes, meetings are **information touchpoints**.

infotisements

These are advertisements that run primarily in email newsletters and appear to be editorial matter, but actually promote a company's products and services. It's a steal from the world of print advertising, which calls them "advertorials."

inner geek

The "techie" deep within each of us. It's what we turn to when we're searching for that abstract clue to help us unlock the secret to our favorite computer game or software program. "If I could just get in touch with my **inner geek**, I could reach the next level."

innovicide

To kill a new idea. "Jack's concept was brilliant, but management committed **innovicide** again."

insourcing

The process of looking inside the company to find someone with the needed skills to perform a certain job. This happens a lot in an economic slowdown. "The budget's tight; we'd better **insource** this one."

Integrity Deficit Disorder

A politically correct term for describing an immoral person.

intellectual infrastructure

The human components — knowledge, skills and abilities — required for businesses and organizations to function effectively. Often used by IT folks when referring to a skilled workforce. "We have the computing power. We just don't have the **intellectual infrastructure**."

The Imglish Dictionary

Imglish is the evolving language of Instant Messaging. It's a collection of abbreviations, acronyms and shorthand that allows IMers to say whole sentences in three to five letters.

BAK Back At the Keyboard

BIBO Beer In, Beer Out

BTDT Been There, Done That

CICO Coffee In, Coffee Out

DOS Dozing Off Soon

DQMOT Don't Quote Me On This

EMFBI Excuse Me For Butting In

FWIW For What It's Worth

GAL Get A Life

GIGO Garbage In, Garbage Out

GMTA Great Minds Think Alike

HUB Head Up Butt

IANAL I Am Not A Lawyer (but …)

IRL In Real Life, which means anytime that you're not online chatting.

MTF More To Follow

NP No Problem, which generally means there is a problem.

OTOH On The Other Hand

OTTOMH Off The Top Of My Head

PAW Parents Are Watching (And you thought your kid was talking about the dog.)

PITA Pain In The Ass

PMFJIB Pardon Me For Jumping In But …

TANTSAAFL There Ain't No Such Thing As A Free Lunch

WYSITWIRL What You See Is Totally Worthless In Real Life

interdependent partnering

"Partnering" has become so overused that in order for it to sound important the BuzzMakers feel compelled to add another layer of obfuscation.

internal community

Consultant-speak for "employees."

Internet speed

You're definitely not cool if your company isn't running at **Internet speed**.

Internut

A term of endearment referring to those whose lives seem to have been consumed by the Internet.

interstitials

Those annoying Web pages, generally carrying ads, that pop up in front of the page you're actually hoping to read.

intrapreneurial

An individual or group effort within a larger organization that takes an entrepreneurial approach to develop new ideas and products, often bucking the bureaucracy in the process. Originally coined by Gifford Pinchot in 1978.

intraview

A formal sit-down with an internal job applicant to discuss his or her qualifications.

inventrepreneur

The new breed of business-savvy inventors, who not only create the products, but also handle the marketing and sales.

issuematic

A user-friendly substitute for "problematic" that attempts to create a positive out of a negative. "Jack's behavior is **issuematic**."

James Bond Effect

Proof that Ian Fleming's 007 is a permanent part of our culture. Used as a description for a multitude of things, from sleek sports cars to high-tech gadgets to sexy women to martinis to tuxedos. "It's a very **James Bond** effect."

jitterati

What the digital generation becomes after sipping one too many cups of Starbucks.

job spill

When work cuts into your personal time.

joe-job

A technique used by spammers to harass a particular Web site or email user by making it seem as if the unsuspecting site is the source of vast quantities of spam. The attacker will send out millions of email messages with the headers forged to appear to come from their victim. Named after the first victim of this type of attack, joes.com.

jump the couch

To lose control or exhibit strange or frenetic behavior. Named for Tom Cruise's couch-jumping antics on The Oprah Winfrey Show.

keepage
The opposite of garbage.

key learnings
An annoying variation of "lessons learned." The recap at the end of a project of what worked and what didn't. Intended to prevent future teams from making the same mistakes.

keyboard dyslexia
Typing all the correct letters, just in the wrong sequence. Occurs often when dashing off an email response.

keypal
Pen pals have faded as the Internet has grown. Email and instant messaging have turned them into keypals. (Keyboards, get it?)

kidult
Adults who "never grew up." They act like kids and revel in being young at heart.

killerbite
A very clever — but very brief — statement. A killer sound bite. Usually uttered by a C-level exec to the media.

kneemail
Religion's effort to give prayer a modern, high-tech image. "God answers **kneemail**."

knowledge transfer
A fancy way of saying "teach someone else how to do your job, so we know what's going on when you leave."

Kremlin-watching
A Cold War pastime with an updated, capitalistic twist. It's the attempt by analysts and the media to read the corporate tea leaves and predict who's being positioned to become a company's future CEO.

krudzu
Any proliferating management fad — or simply dumb concept — that overtakes and eventually strangles a company or organization. Comes from the plant kudzu, which is taking over vast acreage in the South.

kruegerware
A new generation of spyware that hijacks your browser and, like the villain of "Nightmare on Elm Street," can't be killed. It can steal your home page, lock you permanently into a XXX site, or ship all of your Google queries to a dubious ad-driven alternative. And it's next to impossible to get rid of. Like Freddy Krueger, it usually comes back.

kudo loop

The seemingly endless email loop that occurs when everyone in the office feels they must add their 2 cents to that "Great Job!" company-wide email from the boss.

My eyes hurt!

Ozware's new Compliance Automation capabilities automate all aspects of server and application compliance, from granular policy-based auditing with automated remediation to a Compliance Center that includes out-of-the-box reports for Sarbanes-Oxley, ITIL, COBIT and others. Ozware's solution uniquely combines policy compliance capabilities at all layers of the software stack, from operating systems to applications and configurations, with the power of Ozware's Contextual Data Model and unmatched management reach and scalability, allowing customers to achieve truly global automated compliance - an impossible task until now.

ladder up

To get a consumer to the next step in the buying process, to buy more or to "step up" to a premium option. "Once customers make a balance transfer using their new credit card, we want them to **ladder up** to other options."

landspam

Spam delivered by the mailman. Otherwise known as junk mail.

LAQs

A publicist's worst nightmare: Lame-Ass Quotes. In a sound bite world, the last thing you want are **LAQs**.

late bird

Early birds regularly are rewarded with discounts for registering ahead of time, but now event planners are adding official **late bird** sign-up periods for the crowd that habitually misses "final" registration deadlines.

lateral arabesque

To transfer laterally within a company to a different but equal job.

lateraled
To be moved sideways. As in: "I hear you got a big promotion." "No, I got **lateraled**."

lawn mullet
A lawn that's neatly mowed in the front but uncut in the back.

leadager
A person in charge who confuses leadership with micromanagement.

learning opportunity
A great phrase from the spinmeisters that supposedly comforts the stock analysts: It refers to mistakes made that will somehow be turned into future breakthroughs. It's a nice way of saying someone screwed up and we're trying to make the best of it.

legal scrub
To run an idea, contract language, etc. past the corporate lawyers so they can strip out anything that might result in a lawsuit later. "Make sure you give that list of personnel a **legal scrub** before you lay them off."

lessons learned
A $5 phrase for mistakes. **Lessons learned** sessions at the end of projects are generally used by managers to put a positive spin on all the things they screwed up. *See key learnings*

leveraging our assets

An oldie but goodie staple of the modern-day press release. The only folks impressed by the phrase are the insecure CEOs who insist on it being included so everyone will know they're doing their jobs.

lexicurious

To be curious about the meaning or origin of words.

life caching

Collecting, storing and displaying one's life online for friends, family or even the world to see. **Life caching** has been aided by blogs, Web sites, Web cams and camera phones. Result: The world can now see how boring most of our lives really are.

lifestyle enabler

Technology that frees us to do many things while staying connected. Cell phones and Wi-Fi are considered the big "lifestyle enablers." The TV remote is still the BuzzWhacker's favorite.

lifetime value

A corporate measurement that projects how much money a customer will spend with the company over time before defecting and taking his or her business elsewhere.

LIHOM

Acronym for Legend in His (or Her) Own Mind.

limolock

Common occurrence in New York City, where visiting
U.N. dignitaries tie up traffic on the East Side for hours.
A similar phenomenon known as *Bubbalock* occurs every
time former President Bill Clinton goes to lunch.

link farm

A Web site with no meaningful content of its own, just
link after link to other Web sites. They're frequently
created to legitimize what is otherwise a site filled with
affiliate advertising banners.

linkrot

The process of Web hyperlinks going dead. As the
Internet ages, sites die, page URLs change and **linkrot**
sets in. One dead link is annoying. Multiple dead links
indicates **linkrot** and lots of frustrating "Page Not
Found" error messages. *See also* **webrot** *and* **moved to
Atlanta**

lipstick effect

A consumer response to economic hard times. Instead
of purchasing expensive or luxury items (such as
jewelry), consumers buy smaller comfort items (lipstick)
that make them feel good.

living assets

Employees. Could we be any less personal?

lobby lizard

Any person (salesman, groupie, etc.) who camps out in the lobby of an office, hotel, etc. in hopes of meeting the CEO, a rock star, or other luminary.

LOK

Acronym for Lack Of Knowledge. "We're having **LOK** problems again with the computers in customer service."

loop mail

The ever increasing amount of email CCed or copied to you to "keep you in the loop." Most of it is unnecessary, irrelevant and a major reason why you can't get your own work done.

lossy

1) If that digital photo you're looking at looks like it's missing something, you're probably right. It's **lossy**, not glossy. Most digital photos are compressed to save space, so the data is rearranged and it's no longer identical to the original image. It's lost something. They actually call it **lossy** data compression. 2) Reference to someone who has trouble remembering things accurately. "He's **lossy** today."

lunchin'

Crazy or stupid. A shorter version of "out to lunch." "Did you see that guy shoveling snow in his shorts? He's **lunchin'**."

M&Ms
Entry-level employees fresh out of college who fancy themselves "management material." Their candy-coated degree looks great, but inside they melt in the heat of real work.

magnet employer
An employer whose qualities attract job applicants in droves. *See also **heat-seeking workforce***

malicious obedience
Opposite of civil disobedience. A quiet protest of company policy in which employees go through the motions of doing their jobs but intentionally accomplish nothing.

malternatives
Any of the "alternative malt beverages" that have exploded onto the alcoholic beverage scene. Includes "hard" lemonades, fruit coolers and most drinks that have the word "Ice" tacked onto their name. Also known as *alcohol pops* or *alcopops*.

management insultancy
When corporate management hires outside consultants to do what it should be doing — deciding how to run the company! It's an insult to the executives.

managerial courage

Business version of "do the right thing." The willingness to make difficult decisions for the good of the organization, even if they're not in your own best interests.

mandatory fun

A celebratory business event that holds no interest for you but requires attendance since names are being taken.

manny

A male nanny.

marital rupture

Used by those who feel "divorce" needs to sound more clinical. "Julie has suffered through two **marital ruptures** in the past 10 years."

marketecture

A hype-laden description detailing the design and function of a product that frequently exists only in the fertile minds of the marketing department.

marshmallow mining

The practice of digging your hand into a box of Lucky Charms to get the marshmallow tidbits out while avoiding the oat kernels. Variations include *cashew mining* (digging the cashews out of a bowl of mixed nuts) and *M&M mining* (getting the good stuff out of trail mix).

masstige

High-quality products with prestige names at mass-market prices. Long used by fashion and cosmetic companies, it's now the hot marketing strategy for luxury car makers to attract "near-rich" buyers who thought they could never afford a Mercedes, Jaguar or Porsche.

maturialism

Mature consumers' pursuit of the "best of the best" materialism. They're ditching mundane goods and services for more professional, premium or sassier versions. From heavy duty power tools to state-of-the-art cameras to grown-up ice cream flavors. Coined by Trendwatching.com

Maudience

An audience, targeted by marketers, comprised of retired women over 65 who enjoy watching "The Golden Girls."

MBA

To a small part of the workforce, it's a coveted business degree. To the folks who work for bosses with MBAs, it more often stands for Mediocre But Arrogant.

MBWA
Management By Walking Around. When top managers keep in touch with employees by wandering the halls, asking workers what they're working on and getting a clue of what's really going on in the company.

m-commerce
Even though there have been mobile phones a lot longer than there has been the World Wide Web, we're only now getting **m-commerce**. Even then, **m-commerce** can only happen when the phone is connected to the Web. Shouldn't calling up on your cell phone and ordering a pizza be **m-commerce**, too?

meanderthal
Someone who has a difficult time getting to the point when telling a story or giving a presentation. Also: An early riser who wanders aimlessly through the house, unshaven and scratching where it itches.

meatloaf
Unsolicited mass email, circulated by friends or office mates via group email lists, consisting of jokes, anecdotes and other trivia. Where spam is commercial, **meatloaf** is homemade.

meeting moth
An executive who flits from meeting to meeting, but seldom acts on the items discussed in them.

megadigm

A profound change. Coined by change management experts (replacing the less impressive-sounding "paradigm shift") to describe growing customer expectations that managers can no longer ignore.

MEGO

My Eyes Glaze Over. As in: "Reading these buzzword-laden reports triggers a **MEGO** effect."

Mensa-pause

A hot flash caused by deep, profound thinking. "I had a **Mensa-pause** during today's math test."

mental Pez

To be hit with so much information that it becomes impossible to focus on one thing, so stuff goes from top-of-mind to tip-of-tongue, only to eventually fall out of our head completely — the way Pez candy falls out of the head of the dispenser. (From the "Sally Forth" comic strip.)

merchantainment

The meshing of entertainment content with product information. The term was created at Disney World, where staff are trained to be **Merchantainment** Hosts or **merchantainers**. The goal is to create a positive experience for park visitors so they will be inclined to buy more.

mercky

Pharmaceutically dubious. "Data from the Vioxx trials are in and the results appear to be **mercky**." (Merck is a pharmaceutical company that had regulatory issues.)

meta ignorance

Not knowing what you don't know. "At least I have a clue about what I don't know, but my boss suffers from **meta ignorance**."

meta-decision

An all-encompassing, comprehensive decision based on the outcomes of several smaller decisions. "Once all of the smaller issues are resolved, we'll render a final go/no-go **meta-decision**."

microdeckia

Someone who suffers from microdeckia is simply not playing with a full deck of cards.

microwaiting

The time spent in front of the employee break room microwave while your lunch heats up. Regularly occurs a few minutes before noon and is generally not reported as a part of the lunch hour.

migrate

No, you didn't move that data from your old computer to the new one. You **migrated** it.

mismatch-free

The short defintion: match. In the electronics world, a mismatch is the difference between the output impedance of a source and the input impedance of a load. So something **mismatch-free** means there is no difference between the two. Hmm, sounds like a match.

mission-critical

Another sign that too many people in today's business world have read too many Tom Clancy books. What's wrong with the word "essential"?

monetizing eyeballs

It's what ophthalmologists have been doing for years. On the Web, it's a term for figuring out how much each person who looks at your Web site is worth — or is costing you. In today's Internet environment, there's a lot of "monetizing" going on.

monitor-shopping

Online window-shopping. When shoppers surf your Web site — but don't buy.

monopologue

A one-sided "discussion" in which an individual monopolizes the dialogue, giving no one else a chance to get a word in.

MOUSE POTATO

moonshine shop

A place where ideas are distilled and turned into working models in short order. "Boeing's **moonshine shop** works outside the company's traditional channels to develop cheaper, faster ways to build airplanes."

most growable customers

A steal from the agriculture world. Basically, they're customers who could be spending a lot more with you.

motherhood statements

A statement or phrase that no one can disagree with, such as "smoking is bad for you." Politicians regularly use them to make voters feel good — while not having to commit to anything. "I believe in a fair day's wage for a fair day's work!" Big deal. Who doesn't?

mouse milk

Anything that delivers little (or at least hard to measure) payoff — while often requiring lots of hard work.

mouse potato

A person who spends hour upon hour staring into his/her computer screen. Increasingly couch potatoes are giving way to **mouse potatoes**. The TV Generation is losing to the Digital Generation. We're not sure this is really an improvement.

mousing surface
A term for those who feel "mouse pad" lacks cachet.

moved to Atlanta
Slang reference to Web pages that can't be found and generate a 404 File Not Found error message. "404" is the area code for Atlanta, GA. See **404**, **linkrot** and **webrot**

MSM
It may sound like a food additive, but it's blogger shorthand for "mainstream media."

muffin top
The unsightly roll of flesh that spills over the waist of a pair of too-tight low-hanging pants, much like a muffin bursting out of the pan.

muggle
In Harry Potter's world, it's a non-wizard. In the computer industry, hackers are wizards and anyone not in the computer industry is a **muggle**. In the rest of the world, it's simply someone who is mundane.

multiple store-gasms
The ecstasy brought on by hitting as many Christmas sales as possible in a single shopping trip.

multi-slacking

The act (or art) of performing multiple non-productive tasks at once. The best multi-slackers simultaneously talk on the phone, surf the Web and watch TV.

munge

To disguise your email address to make it more difficult for spammers to strip it from newsgroup posts, chat rooms, etc. Example: s0me0ne@example.c0m, using zero instead of an "O." A person can interpret your address, but the automated programs that spammers use can't.

museum kitchens

Beautiful and richly-appointed kitchens primarily designed to impress guests rather than prepare meals.

nagflation

The incessant gloom-and-doom predictions from economic analysts who feel compelled to issue updates even if nothing has changed.

Napsterized

When intellectual property is stolen, copied or shared without the owner or creator getting a cut. Owners of intellectual property are going to great lengths to keep from being **Napsterized**. Photographers add watermarks to their photos, software companies add encryption, and movie web sites make it next to impossible for you to save a film clip to your hard drive. Comes from Napster.com, a site that originally allowed surfers to download music for free.

narcissurfing

Googling yourself to see where and how often your name comes up. See *ego surfing*

NASCAR effect

A collection of award icons, banners, webrings and ads that clutter the bottom or top of a Web page. Like a race car covered in ads, they blur and become meaningless.

negaholic

Someone addicted to negative thinking. "Negaholic specialists," experts who'll help you combat your addiction, say there are at least 14 different kinds of **negaholics**.

negative growth

A positive spin on what is clearly negative and not growth. "After two consecutive quarters of **negative growth**, we think we're poised to succeed."

negative patient outcome

Medical-speak for "the patient died." Often used by hospital bureaucrats and malpractice insurance companies concerned that the death was caused by medical errors.

negative profit

Buzz-speak used to mislead listeners into believing something positive has happened. Pssst! It's a loss.

nerdistan

Any neighborhood or community where a disproportionate number of residents work in high-tech industries. These residents also tend to have a disproportionate number of electrical outlets and phone jacks.

nerdvana

The ultimate state of complete geekiness. Geek heaven. Example: A house with 16 electrical plugs on every wall.

The New Black

Any fashion, style or color that purports to be the next big thing.

New-guy gene

The internal mechanism that triggers extra politeness in new employees until they're up to speed on office politics. Example: "The new guy took the best seat in the breakroom. He totally lacks the **new-guy gene**."

newszak

Newszak once described fluffy TV programs designed to appear as news programming, frequently to promote a product. But now **newszak** is where it really belongs — in the elevator. Flat panel TV screens carrying news, financial updates, and advertising are becoming fixtures in office building elevators all over the country.

next generation

Marketing hype for *next edition* or *next version* in an attempt to make buyers think that what's coming next will be vastly superior to the current iteration.

NIH

Not Invented Here. Frequently results in the discounting of a good idea or product because we didn't think of it.

non-concur

Bureaucratic word choice that allows one to avoid uttering something as definitive as "disagree." The ultimate obfuscation: "Yes, I do not **non-concur**."

NOTE
An anti-development stance that takes NIMBY (Not In My Backyard) to a new level — Not Over There Either.

notwork
For most of us it means to not work. But to a techie, it's a computer network that's flaky or not working. Also known as a *nyetwork* for those with a Russian bent.

now data
The most up-to-the-minute data. "Bob, what's the **now data** on the email campaign's open rates?"

Now Economy
Forget the New Economy, the **Now Economy** has taken its place. It's another swipe at business practices that existed before the Internet rudely interrupted them. The **Now Economy** is so named to reflect that the customer now controls the marketplace, not business. And the customer wants "it" now. And, as the theory goes, they can have it now because of the Internet.

NSTR
Nothing Significant To Report.

NYLON
A New York-London Over Nighter. Someone who lives in New York and commutes regularly to London for business.

O3
Business shorthand commonly used in calendar entries for "Out Of Office."

OBC
Owned by China. The awakening Chinese economy no longer is just the target of outside companies looking for a place to market their goods. Chinese companies are increasingly buying operations in the U.S. and Europe to strut their own brands in the global economy. Such as when China's number one computer maker Lenovo bought IBM's PC hardware division.

office
Thanks to technology, **office** has morphed into a verb. "I'm going to **office** from home today." Or, "I'll manage the New York staff but will **office** out of Atlanta." Kinko's adopted the verbification in an ad campagin: "A new way to **office**."

offline
Primarily, it's wherever you are when you're not on the Internet. But now it has become an office catch phrase heard frequently in meetings. "That's a great idea, but let's deal with that **offline** after the meeting."

ohno-second

The fraction of time (slightly longer than a nanosecond) that it takes to recognize you've just goofed. The perfect example: That moment of horror when your eye spots the key in the ignition as the car door is being slammed shut.

OHOC, OHOT

According to London's Evening Standard, psychologists report that women scanning personal ads are more interested in a man with wealth — **OHOC** (own house, own car) — than one with good looks — **OHOT** (own hair, own teeth).

Olympic tourist

An Olympic athlete with no chance of winning a medal, but who enjoys every moment of just being there.

one throat to choke

The corporate purchasing philosophy of buying or contracting everything (particularly technology solutions) from a single vendor. That way if anything goes wrong, there's only **one throat to choke**.

one-click politics

The ability to vote, share your opinion or make a donation to a political candidate with a click of your mouse. This growing extension of democracy comes with its own flood of political spam (often with bandwidth-eating video messages from the candidates).

one-off
Limited to a single occurrence, such as a one-time event or meeting. The definition has been expanded recently to also mean "one-to-one, offline." As in: "Let's do this **one-off** after the meeting." See *off-line*

online oxygen
The integration of online access into daily life has made a connection to the Internet an absolute necessity — **online oxygen** — for 600 million global consumers.

onshoring
The return of jobs previously "offshored," particularly after a company discovers its customers are frustrated with having to deal with customer service representatives half a world away. See *insourcing*

Open Issues List (OIL)
A favorite of consultants and project management experts, it's simply a list of issues that need to be resolved in order to complete a project. "We can finish this project quickly if we just apply **OIL**."

open-air conference room
An area outside the building where employees convene to discuss business while grabbing a quick smoke. "Let's have this meeting in my **open-air conference room**."

OPEN-AIR CONFERENCE ROOM

operationalize

A weighty-sounding buzz term preferred by consultants that simply means "to implement." "The next phase is to **operationalize** our strategy."

optics

Business jargon for "how things appear."

oranging up

A sign that the weather is getting warmer. It's when the USA Today weather map turns from cool blues and greens to warm yellows, oranges and reds.

organigram

A chart or diagram of a company's organizational structure and hierarchy. And if **organigram** doesn't seem awkward enough, it's often spelled "organogram."

OT-mail

An unnecessary, after-hours email sent to a supervisor or co-workers with the sole purpose of time-stamping how late you worked. Example: An email sent to the boss at 9:24 p.m. — "Just wanted to touch base on the Johnson account. Let me know when we can meet."

out of runway

The point when you realize that no matter how hard you work, it'll be impossible to meet the deadline. "We're almost **out of runway**. If we don't get the report today, we'll never make next week's launch."

over normal
To be above a standard or accepted level. "I don't consider myself fat, I'm just **over normal**."

over-glassed
A building or geographic area with far more fiber optic cable than will ever be needed. Generally the result of either poor engineering or great salesmanship.

overswooshification
To be overexposed in the marketplace. Many think that's happened to Nike, but its swoosh continues to bring in the customers.

over-the-shoulder guidance
Training that promises to be more personal than a seminar or lecture, but less specific than one-on-one instruction. "Our professional services staff are experienced in providing on-site, **over-the-shoulder** guidance and support." Also, some bosses' annoying style of management.

Ozzied, Ozzy'd
An Alzheimer-like condition. The patient can remember the '60s but can't remember what he did two minutes ago. "He's **Ozzied**." A reference to Ozzy Osbourne — poster child for Baby Boomer drug abuse.

pain points
Now the BuzzMakers are stealing from the acupuncturists. Business consultants use **pain points** as a term to describe the places where a business feels the "pain" due to poor operational structure, bad software or good, old-fashioned inefficiencies.

pajamahadeen
The new media watchdogs. Bloggers who spend their days surfing the Net, challenging and fact-checking the traditional media.

paper-form factors
Geek-speak for printed matter, particularly distasteful, old-fashioned things, such as newspapers and books.

paperweight
A useless product or service that does little more than exist. Often thrown in during a sale to give the appearance of "adding value."

paratourist
One who lives in or near a major metropolitan area but still wanders aimlessly or gets lost while touring the area's locales of note. Example: A Chicago **paratourist** would have trouble finding the Sears Tower.

parking lot

A separate sheet of flip chart paper where good off-topic ideas that come up during a meeting are recorded. Supposedly they'll be brought up at a later meeting but are often forgotten altogether.

passing the trash

The practice of transferring a problem employee to another department without alerting the supervisor to the person's objectionable traits.

path persistence

To follow the beaten and established path. For hikers, an intelligent approach that conserves energy. For businesses, a strategy that generally results in loss of market share.

Paula Abduling

1) When two people engage in a duel of opposite opinions — often stooping to personal insults.
2) Giving perky, positive feedback in an effort to spare someone's feelings. "I think she's just **Paula Abduling** me." Derived from Paula Abdul, one of three judges on American Idol, who sometimes argues with the other judges and other times sweet talks contestants.

payroll orphan

Someone who has lost his or her job.

PDFing

Once this term described the process of turning a document into an Adobe PDF (portable document format) file. Now it is a mild curse word, as in: "Where's that **PDFing** document? I had it right here."

peanut-butter spread

The act of taking meager resources (budget, staff, etc.) and spreading them as thin as possible to cover the most projects. "We're gonna have to do a **peanut-butter spread** in Marketing come September."

PEBCAK

An acronym used by techies to describe a "problem" when the user is in the room: Problem Exists Between Chair And Keyboard. *See **PICNIC***

pedanticize

Unnecessary padding to a conversation or document that drags things out and makes it longer than necessary.

pencilator

Meeting facilitator's assistant. Person given the "responsibility" of taking notes on the big flip chart during meetings.

pepper, re-pepper

To "spice up" an existing offer or proposal by giving it a new twist or additional features that appear to add value. "We need to **re-pepper** the proposal."

percussive maintenance

The time-honored art of whacking the heck out of something to get it running again. Long performed on vending machines, it has now migrated to hard drives and computer monitors.

permanent holiday botanical

A fake Christmas tree.

personal coordinates

An individual's contact information: name, address, phone number, email, etc. "Please leave your **personal coordinates** at the tone." Or: "Could you get me Jack's **coordinates**?" *See **contact coordinates***

personal inertia

HR-speak referring to someone's lack of motivation, procrastination or simple laziness. "Jake has **personal inertia** issues."

PFBNB

Paid For But Not Bought. The popular defense chosen by politicians that contends that while they hobnobbed, consulted and took the campaign contributions of unsavory individuals or companies, they're not beholden to them.

PFE

Purpose For Existing. "This purchase aligns perfectly with the company's **PFE**."

PERCUSSIVE MAINTENANCE

PGP

Stands for Pretty Good Privacy, an encryption technology given away free by MIT. Result: It's one of the encryption standards on the Internet. When someone **PGPs** something, they've encrypted it.

phase 2

Once upon a time it actually referred to something that was scheduled to happen during the second phase of a project. **Phase 2** is now more likely a myth and is used to bury new, unwelcome ideas. "That's a great idea for **Phase 2**."

phenomeniche

A marketing phenomenon that appeals to a small niche. Example: Trading Spaces, the TV series. While not a sweeping global phenomenon, it is the undisputed titan of one modest patch of pop culture.

phonesia

1) The affliction of dialing a phone number and forgetting whom you were calling just as they answer.
2) The inability to remember where in the house you left your portable phone.

photox

The process of digitally removing wrinkles and blemishes from a photograph of one's face using Adobe Photoshop or other image manipulation software. Derived from Botox, the wrinkle reducing injections.

PICNIC

Problem In Chair, Not In Computer. Techie-speak for
user error. See **PEBCAK**

ping

To get someone's attention. "We're behind on the
project. Make sure you **ping** Jim to get the ball rolling."
Stolen from the Internet world, where it's a command
that searches to see if an Internet address exists and is
accepting requests. Old timers knew it as the sound
from a submarine's sonar.

planful

A word created by those who think "well-planned" isn't
adequate. A favorite of academics and marketers
(particularly PR execs). "We have to allocate the time of
senior management in a **planful** way."

platform agnostic

You're in technology heaven when your software is
platform agnostic. It means it'll run on any computer
operating system: Linux, Unix, Windows, Mac, etc.

platform diving

You're **platform diving** when you can choose between
the Web, TV, paper, etc. as a delivery method to get
your message or product out. It's another way of
"leveraging" your content.

playlistism

The discrimination of others based on their iTunes playlist.

plowing water

To do something that has no lasting effect, such as working on a project that makes no meaningful contribution. "The CEO says it's important, but in truth we're just **plowing water** to impress the shareholders."

pocket call

The accidental speed-dialing of a friend, spouse or business associate while carrying your cell phone in your pocket. Result: They discover the real you as they listen to 18 minutes of jangling coins and muffled repartee.

pocket of resistance

1) Military term borrowed by business to describe a person or committee that attempts to stall or kill a project by nitpicking it to death or simply letting it die by not returning your calls. 2)What you encounter at your annual review when it's time for the boss to calculate your pay raise.

podfading

What happens to most podcasts. After the initial excitement of producing your own podcast (generally about the 10th show), the thrill wears off and you realize very few people are listening or really care for your efforts. So you just fade away.

politainer

An entertainer turned politician who makes extensive use of his or her entertainment friends and connections in the effort to get elected. (Yes, Governor Ah-nold is an example.)

politically tone deaf

The failure to pick up on cues from those around you. Often caused by arrogance. "The police commissioner was forced to resign, in part because he was **politically tone deaf**."

pop-off

If pop-up and pop-under ads weren't annoying enough, these Web ad nuisances open off-center with the close window buttons unreachable, making them next to impossible to close without dragging them back to the center of your screen.

pop-under

A browser window that opens behind your active one. It usually carries an ad and is considered less annoying than a "pop-up" window, which obstructs the page you've clicked to. This marketing technique only annoys you after the fact.

pop-up retail

A planned "here today, gone tomorrow" marketing strategy. This growing phenomenon uses temporary sales booths in malls or traveling mobile stores to market a product, event or brand for a limited time.

possumist

Someone (generally in upper management) who ignores the truth in the hope that the facts will change or simply go away before disrupting his or her theory.

post turtle

Reference to any dumb person, particularly a politician. When you're driving down a country road and you come across a fence post with a turtle balanced on top, that's a post turtle. You know he didn't get there by himself, he doesn't belong there, he doesn't know what to do while he's up there, and you just want to help the poor stupid thing get down.

potentialize

To strive for maximum potential. Term created using one of the BuzzMakers' favorite techniques — adding "ize" to any noun.

power down

Normal people turn off their computers. Computer geeks **power** them **down**. Sounds far more impressive.

PowerPoint project

Any project where the only thing actually produced was a PowerPoint presentation outlining the project team's original grandiose plans.

PowerPoint software

Strategies, products or services that only exist in a (sales-person's, consultant's, CEO's, etc.) PowerPoint presentation.

PP2P

First, there was P2P (peer-to-peer), the principle of which was embodied by Napster and instant messaging. Now the concept has expanded to include things such as personal digital assistants (PDAs) and digital phones. That's called **PP2P**, personal peer-to-peer.

prairie dogging

A modern office phenomenon. Occurs when workers simultaneously pop their heads up out of their cubicles to see what's going on.

pre-allocate

To allocate something before it's allocated. Huh? Another in the long list of mind-numbing and unnecessary "pre" words.

prebriefing

To brief or prepare someone in advance for a briefing that will occur later. Generally done to keep that person from doing or saying something really stupid during the "real" briefing. Also: A briefing for the media (by a politician's handlers) so reporters will understand what the politician "really means" when he says it.

PRAIRIE DOGGING

prebuttal
A preemptive "counterpoint" to an expected argument. "The Democrats began their **prebuttals** two days before the president's State-of-the-Union address."

preferred customer
Designation that implies special treatment, but primarily means the company has pegged you as someone who buys frequently and pays your bill on time.

pre-integrated apps
Huh? How do you integrate something before it's integrated? Oh, by the way, apps are software applications.

premumble
Opening comments by speakers (or writers) before they begin their real presentations. Hopefully interesting, frequently not.

pre-owned automobile
A brilliant marketing ploy that has convinced millions that instead of buying someone else's problem, they're lucky to be buying a car that's been properly broken in by the previous owner.

presenteeism
When employees are so worried about/devoted to their jobs that they won't leave or take time off — even when it is in their best interests. The opposite of absenteeism.

previously undetected recruiting error (PURE)

Used to describe a recent hire who looked good on paper but has proved to be somewhat lacking once on the job.

preward

A reward given in advance as motivation to tackle a big project.

proceduralize

To formalize a process in writing, liberally adding buzzwords and company acronyms to make it sound far more complicated and important than it really is.

process visually

Can also be said in one word — see. "There was a lot to **process visually** during the opening ceremonies."

productize

To take something that is not a product and turn it into a product. In the tech world, you would turn a raw technology into a marketable product. "We **productized** Jim's code in the new customer service software module."

programmatics

Governmentese for the details of a project or program.

professional learning community
Teachers.

prostitot
A pre-adolescent girl whose dress and manner exudes sexuality — more closely emulating Britney Spears than Shirley Temple.

pseudo variety
Marketing technique by major companies to elbow smaller vendors off store shelves. They extend their brands by creating a **pseudo variety** of similar products made in almost exactly the same way. Example: Budweiser alone produces Bud Light, Bud Dry, Bud Ice, Bud Ice Light, Michelob, Michelob Light, Michelob Dry, Michelob Ultra, Busch, Busch Light, Busch Ice, Natural Light and Natural Ice.

Pulp Pilot
A non-electronic and time-honored method for keeping telephone numbers and addresses. Generally consists of a small, folded piece of paper that can be tucked into a wallet or purse.

purchase paralysis
The inability to buy an electronic gadget for fear the price will soon drop significantly or a new technology will quickly render your gadget obsolete.

purple state
An election battleground state where support appears to be evenly divided between Republicans and Democrats. On election maps, Republican states are generally colored red and Democratic states blue. Hint: Mixing blue and red creates purple.

purpled out
Out of the office. Taken from Outlook calendar, which generates a purple bar when someone is "out of office." "I tried to invite you to the meeting, but you were **purpled out** for the day."

pushback
Feedback, usually negative and requiring reassessment. "Let's float the idea out there and see if there's any **pushback**."

race team

A group of people charged with completing a six-month project in less than two weeks.

radio silent

To refuse public comment on a controversial issue, especially when the answer could be unflattering. "Since Enron they've been **radio silent** on offshore tax shelters." Originated with military vessels that wanted to avoid detection, but now widely used in public relations.

RAK

The unit of measure for Random Acts of Kindness. One random act of kindness equals one **RAK**. "If you commit 30 **RAKs** a month, the world will be a much better place."

rankism

The discrimination by those in power (Somebodies) to intimidate, belittle and invalidate those lower on the social totem pole (Nobodies). Coined by author Robert W. Fuller.

read-only values

Values that are unquestionable, unalterable, non-negotiable. "Drafting a corporate mission statement is largely a search for the company's **read-only values**." Much like "read-only" computer files, which can be viewed but not edited.

realignment program

A corporate euphemism for layoffs. "You've been selected for our corporate **realignment program**."

reBay

To buy an item on eBay only to turn around and sell it on eBay at a higher price.

recipe malpractice

Reminder that just because you know how to turn on a stove doesn't mean you're a chef. "I committed **recipe malpractice** when I added a cup of salt instead of a cup of sugar."

recreational genomics

DNA testing for the fun of it. For $150, ordinary folks can buy a kit (complete with DNA scraper) that will help them trace their ancestry by providing a biologically-based pedigree that shows what extent a person is of European, Native American, African, Asian or Pacific Islander heritage.

10 words or phrases you should never put in a news release

Leading

Virtually every news release claims its company is the leading (put your company's specialty here) in the country. It's not believable anymore. Related words to leave out: Leading edge, bleeding edge, best in class, and Best of Breed (unless you're in the dog business).

Collaborative partnerships

Are we supposed to be amazed? Can you actually have a partnership that isn't collaborative?

Leveraging our assets

Any company that doesn't "leverage its assets" goes out of business. Everyone already assumes you do. Don't waste their time repeating it.

Mission critical

Your product may save us time, reduce errors, solve problems or increase profits, but unless lives are at stake, don't expect the vast majority of people to buy this hype.

Robust

It's a term that best describes coffee. Calling a product robust tells the customer little or nothing. Robustness, a new variation, is even worse. Try spelling out the benefits. It's more effective.

Ultimate experience

For most of us, the "ultimate experience" isn't something that you can put in a press release or publish in a newspaper.

Strategic alliances

Why would you have a business alliance that wasn't strategic?

Actionable

We're tired of actionable steps, actionable results, actionable techniques. Avoid the term unless you have to differentiate those items from the inactionable items you're promoting.

Web-enabled

If you have a Web site and take orders online, just say so. You wouldn't brag about being telephone-enabled or stapler-enabled, would you?

Space

As in "We're in the B2B space."

reefer

If you hear a couple of truckers talking about **reefer** you'll probably conjure up the pungent odor of marijuana. But in today's world, it's likely to be a vital link in the just-in-time economy. **Reefer** is the shorthand term for refrigerated truck or trailer. "They have a whole fleet of **reefers**."

refrigerator art

A business presentation (generally done in PowerPoint) that looks pretty but has little content and even less value. Also refers to the attractive, colorful and expensive bound handouts that accompany such presentations.

refrigerator magnet

A person who can't pass the refrigerator without opening the door and searching for a quick snack.

regurgimailer

Friends and colleagues who forward everything that lands in their in-boxes to everyone they know without checking to see if it's true or even new. "My brother is the ultimate **regurgimailer**. He's always sending urban legends that are at least five years old."

repurposed entree

Leftovers.

reskilling
Techie-speak for retraining. Primarily used by consultants to convince you to pay more for *their* retraining programs.

retailtainment
An "in-store" entertainment event used by the retail world to draw a crowd of potential shoppers. "Hey, Faith Hill is playing over in aisle 3!" (No joke, Wal-Mart really did that.)

retired in place
Describes someone who is in the home stretch of his or her current job or career and is just coasting to the finish line.

retrosexual
The opposite of a metrosexual. A "real" man who doesn't fret about his personal appearance and doesn't really care what others think of him.

reverbiagized
To reword a concept or proposal with the hope of changing the minds of the people who didn't like it the first time around. "It's the same ad campaign, but we **reverbiagized** it."

reverse telecommuting
The act of doing things at work that you should do at home, such as phoning friends, selling stuff on eBay, etc.

RIF
Reduction In Force, the corporate PC term for layoffs. Common usage: "Yeah, Joe's gone; he was **RIFfed**."

ringtone rage
A violent response by cube mates after hearing your annoying cell phone ringtone for the 15th time.

ringxiety
Triggered by the ringtone of a cell phone, it's when everyone in a public place or meeting reaches simultaneously for their cell before it begins it's second embarrassing ring. See *cellular macarena*

RINO
Republican In Name Only. Typically, a Republican who is viewed as being too liberal. A DINO is the Democratic version. See *flag conservatives*

roamed
To be charged roaming fees on your cell phone for calls in areas where you were sure you had coverage. "I got **roamed** and I was calling from home!"

sailboat fuel

Reference used by truckers, pilots, etc., to describe an empty trailer or plane. "He's hauling **sailboat fuel**." Also can refer to someone's intelligence. "He's got **sailboat fuel** for brains."

salad dodger

Someone who is overweight. "What does he look like?" "Well, he's a bit of a **salad dodger**."

salmon day

The experience of spending an entire day swimming upstream only to get screwed and die in the end.

sarchasm

The gulf between the author of sarcastic wit and the person who doesn't get it.

scaremail

Any email circulated en masse that includes the latest "scare," such as LSD-laced postage stamps or needles being placed on gas pump handles, etc. Most are urban legends run amok.

SCLM

Term used by liberals who don't think the So-Called-Liberal-Media is liberal enough. Of course, conservatives call it the "mainstream media."

Scooby snacks

Token compensation, generally non-monetary, given as an award. "All we got for pulling that project out of the fire was **Scooby snacks** — two extra casual days." Taken from the cartoon "Scooby-Doo," where the heroic dog is rewarded with **Scooby snacks**.

scope creep

When a project continues to grow after the contract has been signed. In the end, the vendor does more work than it gets paid for, or the project goes over budget.

screensucking

Wasting time sitting in front any screen — computer, video game, TV. "He missed his deadline because he spent the afternoon screensucking."

screwdriver shop

A "mom and pop" shop where computers are put together with little more than a screwdriver. See **white box**

script kiddies
Computer-savvy teens who search for malicious code (scripts) written by others, tweak it with their own variations, and then (for fun) see how many other computers they can infect with their modified creations.

scrub, scrubbing
In the current climate, **scrubbing** refers to the removal of information or pages from a Web site that could be considered useful to terrorists.

Second.Coming
Although the dot-coms imploded in 2000, e-commerce has exploded since. With the Internet reaching global mass, the **Second.Coming** is upon us. This time the innovative ideas are backed by sound business practices.

security theater
A very public display of security (visible guards, etc.), often used as window dressing to mask the fact that there's actually a lack of security.

self-provision
Buzz-speak for "do it yourself." "They can either **self-provision** or submit a request to the business unit."

SEP
Someone Else's Problem. "Let's outsource production and make it **SEP**."

September 10
Anything that's outdated, old-fashioned or no longer cool. Used to describe the world that existed prior to September 11, 2001. "That dress is so **September 10**."

shake and bake
Something that has its foundations quickly assembled and is then left to its own devices to evolve into its completed state. "Let the project **shake and bake** and see what they turn up." Comes from the Kraft food coating Shake 'N Bake.

sheeple
Have you felt herded lately? Do you blindly go where everyone else is going? **Sheeple** are folks who follow like sheep.

shortening the path to profitability
It's what companies say when they reduce staff size in hopes of putting their companies in the black. "We're not cutting back, we're **shortening the path to profitability**."

shortfalls in compliance
Fancypants word for "screw up." Example: When queried about the mishandling of files regarding a suspect, the FBI spokesperson responded, "Well, we have recently experienced some **shortfalls in compliance**."

shoulder surfer

Someone who tries to peek over your shoulder to steal your password as you withdraw money from an ATM machine or log on to a computer. Or someone you're talking to at a party who keeps looking over your shoulder to find somebody more interesting to talk to.

sidewalk meeting

A meeting held on the sidewalk outside the building where managers make plans, decisions and coalitions — while grabbing a quick smoke. See **open air conference room**

silica-based environmental interface

A window.

silos

Pockets of information isolated in one department of a company and not shared with other departments. Generally this is a limitation of technology, but can also be the result of petty office politics.

silver bullet

In war, it's an infallible attack or defense. In business, it's a guaranteed solution to a problem. In horror fiction, it's what kills the werewolf. And as noted by U.S. Secretary of Defense Donald Rumsfeld, there's no **silver bullet** in the fight against terrorism.

silver ceiling

Management bias that stymies older workers from rising further up the corporate ladder. Instead, younger employees with "potential" get the nod.

simonized

To be verbally bludgeoned, insulted or trashed in a manner similar to the one perfected by American Idol judge Simon Cowell. "Jennifer really got **simonized**."

situ-mercial

A cleverly designed TV commercial that matches the tone and style of the show in which it appears, therefore making it difficult to distinguish where the show ends and the ad begins. (Until the actor quips, "Geico saved me a bunch of money," of course.)

six-inch calibration

Closely related to "percussive maintenance," it refers to lifting a piece of equipment approximately six inches and dropping it onto a hard surface to see if that will make it start working again. See *percussive maintenance*

skilling

The well-timed stripping of assets so as to furnish a getaway. Coined by David Thomson in a Salon.com article in reference to former Enron COO Jeffrey Skilling, who made a **skilling** by cashing in $66 million in stock before resigning.

slacktivism
To engage in some form of activism (political, social, environmental, etc.) from the comfort of your computer or couch.

slaptops
With technology being one of the leading causes of "desk rage," victims are unleashing their frustrations by attacking their office PCs — aptly renamed **slaptops**.

Slashdotted
When a Web site is overwhelmed by a rush of Internet traffic. Named for the deluge of visitors that hammers a Web site after its URL gets posted on a popular Web site such as www.slashdot.org.

sleeper bug
Technology's version of the terrorist sleeper cell. It's a software bug programmed to awaken at a future date and cause havoc.

slivercasting
Thanks to the proliferation of cable and satellite channels, slivercasting — the opposite of broadcasting — is the hottest new thing. Slivercasting allows you to program for the narrowest slivers of the market. So now not only is there a sailing channel, but there is also a slivercast of how to remove ticks from dogs.

sloptions

They're stock options that are not worth feeding to the hogs. After the dot-com crash, there were a lot of **sloptions** out there.

smogging

In sales, it means "blowing smoke" — a hype-laden pitch that makes promises the salesperson can't keep. In California, it's the process of getting your car to pass the state's emissions test.

smotherage

A form of media overkill. When a news organization covers an event (generally of little significance) with multiple reporters, producing stories on every conceivable angle and providing perspectives almost no one is interested in.

SME (subject matter expert)

Once when businesses needed answers, they would go to the appropriate person and "pick their brain." Now those people have an official title: **Subject Matter Expert** or **SME**. Example: When evaluating a new accounting software package, the IS department will go to the accounting department and check with the accounting **SME** to make sure all of the bases are covered.

SMSing

Sending messages from cell phone to cell phone. Users have developed a short and sweet writing style that eliminates letters. AFAIK CU 2NITE. Translation: As far as I know, I'll see you tonight. Also known as texting. The more mundane, technical definition: Short Message System.

SNAG

Sensitive New Age Guy. Describes the ponytail, Birkenstock, Dave Mathews, guitar in the backyard with a big dog, always giving you a hug whether you want one or not type of guy.

snowplows

The early adopters of a new product or technology. As in, "You guys are the **snowplows**. We'll follow once you've worked out the kinks."

socially produced

Describes a Web site that derives its content primarily from a group of unpaid volunteers or visitors to the site who add their two cents worth. Wikipedia is a socially-produced site. *See **wiki***

social software

The core beliefs and norms of behavior that are really what makes a company run. "At EDS, we work hard on our **social software**, because it's at the core of how we get things done."

socialize the idea

To spread an idea with the hope that familiarity will gain it acceptance or build a consensus. Also used as a way of "flying a trial balloon." "Let's **socialize the idea** and see what happens."

SODDI defense

Some Other Dude Did It. A defense team strategy that contends there were ample opportunities for someone other than their client to have committed the crime.

sofa samurai

Someone without military experience (often by making a concerted effort to avoid serving) who now froths at the mouth for war. A modern day chicken hawk.

SOFE

Significant Other Forced Event. Any event your spouse or significant other is obligated to attend — preferably with a date. Pronounced so-fee.

soft copy

An electronic or non-paper copy of a document. The printed version is called "hard copy."

soft skills

Non-technical skills, such as the ability to communicate, problem-solve, empathize, be courteous, etc. Long assumed that these skills are naturally occurring, businesses are only now coming to the realization that some employees lack the **soft skills** to deal with others.

soft-sided luggage

An employee whose talent and multi-tasking abilities allow her to take on assignment after assignment. She seemingly expands, like soft-sided luggage, to handle the workload. Of course, she completely collapses on weekends.

solistening

The act of soliciting information from customers, while listening to their needs at the same time.

solution stack

Techie way of describing a line of products or services that thoroughly address a single (but broad) problem. "We have a comprehensive **solution stack** that includes the technology, services and knowledge critical to protecting our customers' interests."

songlifting

It's definitely not uplifting. **Songlifting**, a cross between song and shoplifting, is the act of illegally downloading music.

space

As in "we're in the _____ **space**." Fill in with your favorite industry, business model, vertical marketplace, etc. Most commonly heard these days is "B2B **space**."

space junk

The space-eating files on a computer that you suspect no longer have a purpose but are afraid to delete.

spaghetti test
To throw against the wall to see if it sticks. In business, it's to throw out an idea or proposal to see if it's accepted.

spam count
The ratio of legitimate email to spam. "Since I started using a spam filter, my **spam count's** higher than ever. Go figure."

spamish
The insertion of symbols, numbers and spaces into words in an effort to fool today's more sophisticated spam filters. Result: Sp&m g@ts throu?h the f!lters & !nt0 y0ur mai1b0x. And you still can understand it.

spammified
When a legitimate e-mail ends up your spam folder. This has become the digital world's hottest excuse. "Sorry, I just got your message. It was spammified."

spam-o-grams
Those free email holiday greeting cards sent in bulk by "friends" who don't think you're worth the price of a stamp.

spamvertise
To advertise by using spam. In most cases, the word spam alone is sufficient to describe such a practice.

special sauce

Business jargon referring to anything considered proprietary. "In the benchmarking study, they openly discussed everything except the **special sauce**." Comes from the mysterious **special sauce** on a Big Mac.

Spin Room

The room backstage following a presidential debate where spokesmen for each candidate are readily available to the media to explain what each candidate "really" said.

spinach cinema

A movie that's supposedly "good for you," but you dread having to see.

spin-up

To bring someone "up to speed" on the latest events or issues. "We'll need to **spin-up** the new CFO on the irregularities the auditors found." The phrase originally was applied to starting up a hard drive.

SPIT

First there was spam. Then SPIM (SPam by Instant Messenger). Now get ready for **SPIT** (SPam over Internet Telephony). It may not be a problem yet, but two companies have already filed patents to fight this new form of voicemail spam.

splog
A fake blog created by spammers as a home for their ads and scams. Of the 7,000 new blogs started each day, nearly 10% are now **splogs**.

SPOD
Spinning Pizza Of Death. Apple Macintosh equivalent of the Windows hourglass icon. Indicates that the computer is working and working and working and working . . . Also spelled **SPoD** by really hip geeks.

Springer
A reference to the element of society that so often seems to be a guest or audience member of the Jerry Springer TV talk show. Examples: "I could have gotten it cheaper at Kmart, but I'm not into dealing with the **Springer** crowd today." "She's a nice girl, but have you seen her family? Very **Springer**."

squeeze & tease
The practice of shrinking and pushing aside the closing credits of a TV program to promo an upcoming show in order to keep your eyes glued to the screen and your hand off the remote control.

squirt the bird
Upload data or info to a satellite. This one's been around a long time, but with the growing acceptance of satellite TV and satellite radio, we're **squirting the bird** a whole lot more these days.

stall talker

The annoying person sitting in the next bathroom stall who decides it's a great time to strike up a conversation. Also someone who talks on his or her cell phone while using a public restroom.

Starsky

The person in every office who regularly volunteers to take control of the mouse or click the slides for someone else's demonstration or presentation. From the 1970s cop series and 2004 movie "Starsky and Hutch," where Starsky always drove the car.

starter castle

A large house built on a lot so small there's no room for the moat. Generally resented by the neighbors for its ostentatious display of affluence — and frequently bad taste.

starter marriage

In the U.S., the **starter marriage** has become the norm. It's a short-lived first marriage that ends in divorce with no kids, no property — and no regrets.

stateau

A statistical plateau, as in "Barry Bonds reached the 700 home run **stateau** in 2004."

staycheck

It's what struggling companies give employees to guarantee there'll be someone left to turn out the lights. Everywhere else it's called a paycheck.

stealth parenting

The practice of claiming you have a business appointment or breakfast meeting to hide from a less-than-understanding boss the fact you are really taking your kids to school.

Stepford

In research focus groups and testing, a **Stepford** is a participant who is too eager to please. "That one isn't going to give honest feedback, she's too **Stepford**." Also: A sports fan who blindly supports a team, never questioning or doubting the wisdom of team management. "Flyers fans are real **Stepford** fans." From the sci-fi film, "The Stepford Wives."

Stepford crowd

A handpicked or invitation-only crowd chosen to give the appearance that a political candidate has broad and enthusiastic support from the electorate.

sticky

Trait of Web sites with content that's interesting enough that you stop and read it.

straight to video

In Hollywood, it's to forego a theater release and market the movie directly to the home market through rentals and sales. On the dating scene, it's someone you'd entertain at home but wouldn't want to be seen squiring around town.

strategery

After being coined by Saturday Night Live writers to poke fun at George Bush, one group of presidential advisors with a sense of humor named themselves "The **Strategery** Group." Now it seems every talking head on TV uses **strategery** without realizing there's no such word.

strategic alliances, strategic partnerships

Why would you have a business alliance or partnership that wasn't strategic? "Our **alliance** with ABC Company was **strategic**, but our **partnership** with Zippit Co. was just for fun!" No, you won't hear that.

strategic ingratiation

Brown-nosing, sucking up. "I need that raise, so I'm going to engage in a little **strategic ingratiation** by volunteering for that extra assignment."

streaking

Connecting to the Internet without a firewall, virus protection or spyware protection, which is about as stupid as the '70s campus craze for which it's named.

stretch goal

A target so far beyond the seeming capabilities of a group or company that it appears at first to be impossible. Of course, it often still appears impossible to achieve at project's end, too.

subject creep

The tendency for an email list or newsgroup discussion to veer off topic while the subject line remains the same.

success virus

Updated version of "success breeds success." In companies, it occurs when a single small success buoys the staff in such a way that it spreads like a virus, leading to a series of "wins."

Sudden Paycheck Detachment Syndrome

The numbing depression caused by suddenly losing your job. Coined by Kevin Mireles, who launched his own job-hunting Web site (FindKevinaJob.com) after suffering **SPDS**.

Sudden Reputation Death Syndrome

Occurs when top execs with sterling reputations (or at least darlings of Wall Street and the media) stumble, triggering a downward spiral that gets them booted. Coined by Fortune magazine. Examples: Jeff Skilling at Enron, Jacques Nasser at Ford.

suite of options

A favorite in the technology world. Users no longer have choices, menus or options, they have a **suite of options** — thanks to the "suite of tools" made available by a "suite of programs."

surfer's voice

The inattentive, half-hearted tone (punctuated with surreptitious tapping of a keyboard) that means the person on the other end of the phone is more focused on surfing the Web, reading emails and trading instant messages than listening to you. *See* ***IMpause*** *and* ***EMV***

SWAG

Swag has a lot of legitimate definitions. Pirates' booty was called **swag**. And the promotional freebies marketers hand out at trade shows are **swag**. But the buzzword we're referring to is an acronym. You **SWAG** it when you need some quick, ballpark numbers to back up your new product idea. How much will it cost? How much revenue will it bring in? Stands for: Scientific Wild Ass Guess or Systematic Wild Ass Guess.

swankoplex

A cinema multiplex with a "first class" seating section (with extra wide leather chairs), cocktail lounge, restaurant and concierge service. The first one, naturally, was in L.A.

sweet spot
Another sports term that has migrated into business. In sports, it's the part of the bat, golf club, tennis racquet, etc., that provides the best hit. "I hit it in the **sweet spot** and the ball just sailed." In business, the meaning is similar. Example: Pricing in the **sweet spot** means setting the price where it achieves the most profit.

swiped out
An ATM or credit card that no longer works because the magnetic strip is worn away from overuse.

Swiss-knife effect
To be overly impressed with a product's fancy bells and whistles.

sympvertising
Advertising that sympathizes with the plight of consumers in the hope of selling them something. Example: "Recession Special: 2 dogs and a drink for $1.95."

synlapse
A neural transmission problem when, in your "Golden Years," you find yourself in the kitchen and can't remember why. A modification of synapse. See **destinesia**

tacit knowledge

A buzzwordy way to describe the knowledge an employee has from his experience working at a company. The Holy Grail of today's "knowledge management" systems is to capture an employee's **tacit knowledge** so that know-how can be retained in case the employee bolts the company.

taffy task

A task or job that only takes five minutes, but is stretched to take up the entire day. Frequently used on Mondays and Fridays, when you really don't feel like doing anything, but still need to look busy.

take-away

The main point(s) to remember from a conversation, document, speech, meeting, etc. "It was a great meeting. Too bad there was no **take-away**."

take-away tableware

Fancy-pants talk for plastic forks, knives and spoons. "Sorry sir, we don't have **take-away tableware** to go with your doggie bag."

talking hairdo

A TV journalist concerned more with appearance than the substance of his or her reporting.

talking in real time

This is something that we don't seem to do much of these days. It means actually talking to someone, rather than emailing, text messaging, leaving voicemail, etc.

Targasm

Tingly sensation shoppers get when they find something really, really good at Target.

Tarzan

To make a bold leap, grabbing a sometimes moving target from which to make another, similar leap. "As long as they're able to **Tarzan** through these financings from vine to vine, they're in good shape."

task-saturated

To be overwhelmed with too many things to do at once. "Jack's **task-saturated**. He's got seven projects due Friday." Borrowed from the military, where it generally refers to personnel in a crisis situation, such as a pilot trying to save a crippled aircraft.

taxi moms

Moms who spend most of their day shuttling kids from one lesson, practice, event, etc., to another. While the mini-van targeted soccer moms, an ad from Hummer targets **taxi moms**.

TCO

The Total Cost of Ownership, which includes not only a product's price but the salaries of the staff required to run and maintain it.

Techniban

A fundamentalist mindset (think Taliban), opposed to new technologies that could upset the status quo.

telepathetic

Description of a person whose predictions or guesses are more often wrong than right.

telephonically communicated

To convey information or data by telephone. "The results of the retest were **telephonically communicated** to the CEO." A less buzzy alternative: "I called Jack."

templatized

Any work or job that's had the creativity sucked out of it and has basically been reduced to filling in the blanks.

terrestrial radio

What most of us knew simply as "radio" before there was satellite radio, Internet radio, podcasts, etc.

texters

People who obsessively send text messages via cell phones. Of course, in that world it's spelled TXTRS.

thanking you in advance

An annoying phrase that expresses less-than-sincere gratitude while assuming you will do what is being requested. Long considered an offensive cliché, it continues to proliferate, particularly in business correspondence.

therapeutic reboot

The practice of shutting down and restarting a computer as part of its regular maintenance. "**Therapeutic reboots** will keep your computer from crashing as often."

therapize

To give or receive therapy. "He's been medicated and **therapized**, but nothing seems to help."

thin-brained

This one's been around awhile, but appears to be a favorite of Microsoft's Bill Gates. A not-so-polite way of calling you a mental midget.

thin-slicing

To make a quick decision based on very little data (a thin slice). We used to call them first impressions.

thought parsing

To filter online blogs in a manner that allows you to see what others are thinking (or at least writing).

thought shower

Brainstorm.

thread count

Originally a textile term indicating the quality of the fabric. The higher the **thread count**, the higher the quality. Now used to indicate perceived quality of nearly anything. "The consultant is expensive, but her work is high **thread count**."

threadmates

Fellow denizens of an online message board or discussion list, who share similar interests and opinions. "I can't wait to see what my **threadmates** on the Cruciverbalist list have to say about this."

Three Finger Salute

Another name for Control-Alt-Delete, the command of last resort that allowed early PC users to restart their computers when they froze up.

thrifted

Removal of a product feature in order to save money. "The power liftgate on the van was **thrifted**." Also: To buy from a thrift store. "I **thrifted** my way to a new wardrobe."

throw it over the wall
The process of passing a problem from one department to another — usually reserved for workplaces that house their workers in cubicles (cubes).

thrown under the bus
When a co-worker drags your name through the mud. To be made a scapegoat. "Jackson got **thrown under the bus** by his own teammates."

ticker shock
That numbing feeling investors get as they watch the Dow Jones and NASDAQ averages plummet.

tick-tock
Moment-by-moment developments. Minutiae. "We're trying to stay focused on the Big Picture, not the **tick-tock**." In journalism parlance, it's a story that recounts minute-by-minute the breathless details of a single event.

time frame
The pompous way of giving an approximate date. These folks don't finish projects "sometime in June," they finish them "in the June **time frame**."

time toilet
Any project, assignment, meeting, etc., that takes more time than expected — effectively flushing away your day. "I would have finished the report last week if Frank hadn't called that **time toilet** team building session."

timeboxing
A project management tool that forces you into a mindset of "I'm going to do the best possible job in this fixed amount of time," rather than "I'm going to do the best possible job no matter how long it takes."

tin kickers
Nickname for aviation disaster investigators, who are known for their ability to tease clues from mangled bits of metal. "We have no idea what caused the crash. It's up to the **tin kickers** now."

togethering
Vacationing or traveling with a group, particularly your extended family. "This summer we'll be **togethering** with Biff's family on Cape Cod."

toner phoner
A telemarketing scam in which the caller poses as a sales rep from your regular office supply company offering copier/printer supplies at cut-rate prices "if you buy now." Often the "supplies" never arrive, but your credit card is charged.

topic tiling
The practice of projecting the topic or key points of a speech repeatedly onto a backdrop behind the speaker as if brilliant phrases such as "Corporate Responsibility" or "Strengthening the Economy" will keep you riveted to your seat.

touchpoints

This might sound erogenous, but it's not. In business, it's every point where the company and its products and services come in contact with the customer. Marketers and politicians have become obsessed with controlling every **touchpoint**.

tourists

People who use training classes as a way to get a vacation from their jobs. "We had 10 serious students in the class. The rest were just **tourists**."

traction

What Firestone lacked, but other businesses seem to want. **Traction** means to gain ground. Examples: "We're getting **traction** in the B2B space." "The new sales campaign has **traction**."

transcreate

Simply translating a Web site into other languages isn't enough. When the Chevy Nova was marketed in Latin America, Nova was translated to No Va, which means "no go." So now **transcreating** is the big thing. Instead of a verbatim translation, copy is massaged and rewritten to convey the proper meaning.

treeware

Any paper-based printed material, such as newspapers, books, etc. In techie circles, it generally refers to documentation manuals.

trickle-down ergonomics

The practice of stealing (or being given) an Aeron chair, desk, computer or other workplace goodies after you've been laid off.

truthiness

Something that has the ring of truth to it, that you may even want to be true, but has no real basis in fact.

tszuj

To tweak, finesse or make better (pronounced zhoozh). Another term from "Queer Eye for the Straight Guy" that's found its way into business lexicon. "If we **tszuj** distribution, we should be able to reduce costs."

tunneling

Refers to top executives transferring assets and cash out of a corporation into their own private accounts, leaving the company primarily with liabilities and assets of little value. Thanks to Adelphia, Tyco and others for bringing this term to our attention.

twit filter

Most email programs come with one. It lets you separate your email by name, address, subject line, keywords, etc., so you can filter the "twits" from your favorite email discussion list. Works well with spam, too.

two-comma

Denotes anything that costs $1,000,000 or more. "The new server configuration is a **two-comma** project."

typerventilating

An instant messaging panic attack.

typosquatter

Someone who reserves a domain name one letter off of a famous name in hopes of stealing orthographically-challenged customers. For example, if you want to read the Washington Post online but accidentally type in www.washingtonpst.com, you'll be whisked to a site that sells magazine and newspaper subscriptions.

undertooled

Lacking the proper tools to do the job — whether it's the correct wrench or a college degree. "Without an MBA, I'm **undertooled** for that position."

uniques

Sounds like the name of a '50s rock 'n' roll band — Johnny and the Uniques. Actually, it is the number of **unique** visitors to a Web site. "Sure, their ad rates are lower, but their site doesn't get nearly as many **uniques** as ours."

upgrade the herd

To hire better people and/or weed out the bad ones. "Smart companies are using the down economy as a chance to **upgrade the herd**."

uplevel

Corporate-speak for raising or taking something to a new level. "We'll need to **uplevel** our thinking for this client."

upskilling

To develop new skills, generally technical ones — often by reskilling (retraining). See *reskilling*

UPTITLING

up-titling

The practice of giving impressive-sounding titles instead of raises. Examples: The Head of Verbal Telecommunications is really a receptionist. An Optical Illuminator Enhancer cleans windows. And Stock Replenishment Executives stock shelves.

value-added

The cornerstone of modern marketing, it's a business practice that closely resembles sleight of hand. Simply stated, a company tacks on extra features (service, warranties, additional products, etc.) to its product so the customer has difficulty comparing prices with the competition.

value proposition

The angle a company uses to pitch its products. How fast can a **value proposition** change? Try overnight. The Apple Mac mini gave us a great example. On Feb. 27, 2005, the Apple Mac mini Web site blasted Intel-based PCs because their integrated Intel graphics chip steals power from the CPU. PC owners would have to buy a separate graphics card just to match the Mac mini, Apple boasted. The very next day, Feb. 28, those very same integrated Intel chips became Apple's new **value proposition**: "Mac mini features a graphics processor integrated into the system, and one that's no slouch, to boot. The Intel GMA950 graphics supports Tiger Core Graphics and the latest 3D games. It shares fast 667MHz memory with the Intel Core processor, for an incredible **value proposition**."

vampire creativity
Marketing term for a commercial that is so creative and entertaining that people remember the ad, but not the product being sold. It essentially bites itself.

vapor trail
The tell-tale sign of a co-worker who uses too much (and likely cheap) cologne or perfume. The lingering odor can be detected long after he's passed by.

vaporware
Software (and sometimes hardware) that has been announced (or intentionally leaked) but doesn't exist yet. At its worst, **vaporware** is a marketing ploy where a company announces the undeveloped software as a way to keep its customers from bolting to the competition's latest release. Preferring to simply upgrade over switching to a whole new system, most customers will wait. Then the company scrambles to make the product a reality. This is usually followed by several announced delays to "work out the bugs." More than likely it'll still be buggy when it finally ships.

variable staff
Additional folks to do the job. They can be part-time temps or full-time employees borrowed from other departments to cover an increase in workload. "The fixed staff is 18, but in the summer we need 20 **variable staff**."

vehicular circulation
Traffic.

vendor agnostic
A solution or idea that does not require the use of any particular vendor in order to work. Also, a consultant who steers clear of endorsing any software or vendor.

vendorware
Freebies, such T-shirts, hats, bags, etc., imprinted with a company logo. Usually given away at trade shows and worn by slobs who have no intention of actually ever buying anything from the vendor. Sometimes spelled *vendorwear*.

verbicidal
Condition that exists when a person believes he or she is skilled in the use of words (a verbalist), but in reality is grammatically challenged.

verbing
Corporate America's favorite pastime — the practice of turning perfectly good nouns into verbs. Example: "We're transitioning to the new building in April, just after we finish databasing the surveys."

versatilists

Multi-skilled people who are experts in more than one field. "We're now in pursuit of **versatilists** rather than generalists or specialists. Not only can they write great marketing copy, but they can design the product, too."

vertical evacuation

To move to a higher floor (or higher ground). Heard frequently the past few years as the Gulf Coast has been pounded by hurricanes.

viewshed

In national park parlance, it's the technical term for whatever you can see from a given spot. To the tourist stopped at an official overlook, it's simply "the view."

virtualing

Sounds like something you should do at an Internet séance. It's what happens when one Web server reaches into the database of another Web server and retrieves information stored there.

virtual visitation

When a divorced parent uses a Web cam or other technology to "visit" his or her child.

visioning

One buzzword to replace another buzzword. Instead of "brainstorming," it's now **visioning**.

v-mail

E-mail with only one purpose — to spread a virus. "Lately I've gotten more **v-mail** than email." This definition is quickly being replaced with "video email."

voluntold

When your boss volunteers you for a committee or project assignment without checking with you first.

vortal

First there were Web pages, then Web sites, then Web directories, which morphed into Web portals. Now some portals have gone vertical and have become **vortals**. Where portals were general gateways to the Internet with lots of links to interesting things, news and search engines, **vortals** serve a specific niche, such as an industry, job function, even hobbies.

voted off the island

To get booted from a team, task force or committee. Also, to get fired or laid off. "Jack no longer works here. He got **voted off the island**." Borrowed from the TV show Survivor, where contestants vie to be the last voted off the island.

VSP

Corporate-speak for buyout. The Voluntary Separation Program offers Voluntary Separation Packages (financial incentives) to encourage employees (hopefully older and higher paid) to voluntarily leave so a company can reduce the workforce and lower expenses.

vuja day

The distinct feeling you've NEVER been here (or heard this) before. The opposite of deja vu. "That new ride at Cedar Point was major **vuja day**, dude!"

Vulture Capitalists

Before the dot-com crash, venture capitalists were considered angels. Afterward, they earned their new moniker by turning on their digital babes.

walled garden

A restricted area within a Web site where only "members" may go. Widely used by sites ranging from nytimes.com to porn sites. The sites generally have some free content, but to get the "good stuff" you must either register or pay a fee.

wallet share, share of wallet

At some point, trying to increase market share gets expensive. So, companies go after a bigger share of your wallet. Example: Since you can only consume so many colas a day, a soft drink company will try to increase its share of your wallet by selling you peanuts or chips produced by another division of its company.

wanding

The process of being searched at airport security stations with a metal-detection wand.

war normal

What passes for normal under the conditions of a nation at war against terrorism: heightened security everywhere, a stagnant economy, layoffs, increased anxiety, etc.

warchalking
Symbols used by wireless hackers, usually drawn on walls or sidewalks, to mark nearby wireless networking nodes that can be tapped into for free. Reminiscent of the symbols hobos once used to mark safe places to sleep or where they could get a free meal.

warm-chair attrition
The drop in productivity that begins when an unhappy worker checks out mentally and ends when he or she finally finds a new job and quits.

warspying
Video eavesdropping. Electronic peeping toms, armed with mobile video receivers in their cars, ride around town scanning for wireless video cameras to tap into. Also known as *video sniffing*.

watercooler effect
Buzz created by news or an event (generally non-work related) that sweeps through an office, distracting the employees and bringing work to a crawl.

wave rat
Describes someone who tried to turn the tsunami tragedy into a quick buck.

Web rage

When Net frustration turns into violence. Most harmless form: A computer monitor gets whacked. Most serious: A cubicle mate gets whacked. Chief causes: Slow-loading Web sites and unhelpful help buttons.

Web-enabled

Ducks are web-enabled. But it seems now if you use the Web to do business, you're **Web-enabled**. That means you've been telephone-enabled, stapler-enabled and spreadsheet-enabled for years.

webify, webification

The magic that occurs when executives tell the Web team to add some content to the company Web site. "Can you **webify** this graph for me?" Or "Let's give this document to Tom for **webification**."

weblift

Cosmetic surgery comes to the Net. A **weblift** describes the process of redesigning a Web site to give it a new look and feel. If you're using a consultant, it's a lot more expensive than a facelift.

webliography

A collection of URLs or Web site links that provide easy access to information related to a given subject. Aren't you glad the buzzmasters didn't name it urliography?

wet signature

An original signature. The old-fashioned kind, written in ink on a real paper document — not one that's been faxed, photocopied or scribbled electronically with a stylus.

wetware

There's hardware, software, vaporware, etc., but behind it all is wetware. It's literally the human brain. Can also be used to refer to the human beings (programmers, operators, managers, etc.) who actually run computers. "Our mainframe would be nothing without our **wetware**."

WFH

Abbreviation for "Working From Home." Generally spotted in email subject lines from colleagues who've decided at the last minute they're going to "work from home" (wink, wink) that day.

whacking

Short for wireless hacking. Targets: Your digital phone, personal digital assistants, wireless computers, etc.

whale tail

The top rear strap of a woman's thong, which closely resembles a whale's tail rising from the water whenever the wearer bends over or squats.

wheel estate

Generally a derisive term for mobile homes, but may also be used to describe RVs (recreational vehicles).

white box

A generic personal computer assembled and sold by small "mom and pop" manufacturers. The PC casings are generally cream white and are often packed in unlabeled white boxes. "We're so cheap we could only afford to buy **white boxes**." *See **screwdriver shop***

white collar spam

Unsolicited email sent by legitimate companies that think they have a relationship with you even if you're sure they don't.

whiteboard

The act of brainstorming by listing ideas on a large write-on/wipe-off board. "Let's **whiteboard** the new product launch in the conference room at 10 a.m."

whitelisting

Opposite of blacklisting. Creating a list of people or companies you'll accept email from. To reduce spam, people are using Internet **whitelisting** services to filter their email.

white space
The unmet needs of a customer. The space that is filled by no other product or service. In other words, if you want to make a million as an entrepreneur, all you have to do is find the **white space** – and fill it.

whortal
An Internet portal that liberally trades Web page real-estate and traffic for revenue, without long-term concern for user experience. Imagine that! A company prostituting itself for short-term gains.

wigglespace
The 21st Century update of "wiggle room." "We built in some **wigglespace** to make sure we wouldn't miss the deadline."

wiki
A collaborative Web site or online effort, where many people contribute to the site's content. Wikipedia is such a site. Wiki comes from the Hawaiian word "wiki wiki," which means "quick." *See* **socially produced**

wire frame
A rough draft or idea. "Once we get the **wire frame**, we'll develop the rest of the plan."

WOCAS

The operating philosophy that made Amazon the great customer service success it is. Stands for: What Our Customers Are Saying.

WOMBAT

Someone or something that's a "Waste of Money, Bandwidth and Time."

WOOFs

Well-Off Older Folks.

word-of-mouse

Here's a real down-to-earth term for viral marketing. See the "Tell a Friend" button at the top of a Web page? Click it, fill in your friends' names, and you'll be committing **word-of-mouse**.

work spasm

The initial spurt of energy you pour into work after returning from vacation or a relaxing weekend. It generally wears off by lunch on Monday.

workflower

Someone who blends into the background at work. Example: After two years, you suddenly notice that the mousey blonde you keep passing in the hall works with you.

working off the side of your desk

To be so overloaded with work there's no more room left on your desktop. "I'd like to help you out with that project, but I'm already **working off the side of my desk**."

Workplace Services

Trendy name that's replacing "Human Resources Department," which was the trendy name that replaced the "Personnel Office."

works as designed

A common rejoinder, often used by engineers and programmers, to a flawed product. "Can't help you. It **works as designed**." Of course, the Titanic worked as designed, too. Designed to stay afloat if two compartments were flooded, it sank when three were breached.

world-first technology

Marketing hype used to make a new advancement in technology seem even more significant. The new marketing favorite replaces phrases such as "leading edge" and "cutting edge."

Yetties
Young, entrepreneurial, tech-based twentysomethings. Also known as "young, entrepreneurial technocrats."

YMMV
Internet-speak for "Your Mileage May Vary." A disclaimer often used in email discussions and message boards when stating your experience or giving your opinion. "Of course, this is just my experience, **YMMV**."

yogurt cities
Cities with thriving "active cultures" — museums, symphonies, opera, independent bookstores, etc. — where baby boomers will choose to retire (instead of retirement communities).

YOYO
Acronym for You're On Your Own. Commonly used in text messaging and in chat rooms, but increasingly slipping into daily business discourse. "Wish I could help more, but my expertise is coding. YOYO."

YYSSW
A text-messaging shorthand term that personifies the Y-generation. "Yeah, Yeah, Sure, Sure, Whatever."

zero install

Software that can be accessed through the Web and doesn't need to be installed on every worker's computer — much to the delight of the IT department.

zerotasking

To do nothing or have nothing to do. Taken from the caption of a New Yorker cartoon, which pictures a serene-looking man plopped in a comfy chair.

zitcom

A television situation comedy (sitcom) for teenagers — perfect for marketing acne remedies.

zombience

The atmosphere of a fine establishment that has all the trappings of elegance and the promise of great service, yet employs a staff that resembles the living dead.

BuzzWhackers who contributed to this book

Aaron Alward
Aaron Levine
Aashish Sharma
Adrienne Lewis
Alan Batts
Alan Johnston
Alan Skolnick
Allen Crosby
Allen Danielowsk
Amado Izaguirre
Ambrose Alward
Amy Eisman
Amy Hoy
Ananth Srinivas
Andreas Steude
Andrew Collins
Andrew Graham
Andrew Hargreave
Andrew Kirkwood
Andrew Lord
Andrew Penchuk
Andrew Smith
Andrzej Olszewski
Andy Siegel
Anil Gangs
Ann Olson
Ann Pence
Anna Lee
Anna Sterling
Anne McKay
Aole Wright
Arlyn Moulder
Ashley Bogle
Audrey Byrnes-Tolley
Banning Cohen
Barb Friedman
Barbara Miller
Barbara Wilson
Bart Liddon
Bernie Corrigan
Beth Camero
Beth Wegerbauer
Bette Sweet
Bill Albrecht
Bill Burke
Bill Foley
Bill Garcia

Bill Morris
Bill Wrbican
Billy McCormac
Bob Cloutier
Bob Cockrum
Bob Fegan
Bob Garrett
Bob Morrell
Bob Ralian
Bob Shier
Bob Wiley
Brenda Friedman
Brenda Wakeman
Brent Bailey
Brett Cunningham
Brian Finnegan
Brian Goodwin
Brian Hoag
Brittani Mauldin
Bron de Wein
Brown Brooks
Bruce Watermeyer
Bud Porter-Roth
Cade Bryant
Carl Dreyer
Carl Standish
Carol Bradbury
Carol Katarsky
Caroline Mackersey
Carolyn Neilson
  Brooks
Casey Neese
Charles Baker
Charles Henderson
Charles Mitchell
Cho Ullas
Chris Andrews
Chris Boivin
Chris Caggiano
Chris Clarke
Chris Hereford
Chris Lange
Chris Rock
Chris Siegel
Chrisa Hickey
Christine Patrick
Christopher Forsyth

Christopher Paulin
Christopher Simpson
Christopher Uren
Chuck Young
Claire Colvin
Clifton Griffin
Clive Keen
Colin Dunn
Colleen Kingsbury
Craig Hughes
Craig Ogan
Curt Wieden
Curtis Harkins
Dale Riley
Dan Marchant
Daniel Deal
Daniel Hall-Stith
Daniel Morin
Daniel Wang
Dave Anderson
Dave Brooks
Dave Farrant
Dave Fisher
Dave Jilk
Dave Linabury
Dave Roberts
Dave Sorgen
Dave Worthen
David Askren
David Atherton
David Bogenhagen
David Byers
David Fevre
David Hatchuel
David Hilary
David Kingsley
David Lee
David Manthey
David Miller
David Roberts
David Ross
David Schwab
David Taylor
David Vanderschel
David Walker
David Wellons
Dean Duncan

Debbi Swanson
Debbie Gassmann
Deidre Moore
Dennis Davis
Deon Blair
Derek Moyer
Deri Reed
Diane Walkowiak
Dick Stenmark
Don Steffen
Don West
Dror Eyal
Dunn Miller
E. Haydin
E. Lachaine
Earline Hughes
Ed McKendry
Ed Nicholson
Edward Bania
Edward Becker
Edward Petitt
Eileen Blass
Elizabeth Dinan
Elizabeth Shaw
Ellen Martin
Eric Dahlinger
Eric Gollihar
Eric Hale
Eric Nagle
Eric Smitty
Erik Bergman
Erik Talgoy
Esther Smith
Ethan Hirsh
Evan Schnittman
Eve Oey
Fabrice Bergez
Frank Elfring
Frank Shernoff
Franz Krachtus
Fritz Liess
Fuller Karricker
G. Johnson
Gail Felipe
Garrick Herrmann
Gary Frey
Gary Wollin

Gavin Wilson
Gene Newman
George Wingard
Geri Modell
Gert-Jan Blaas
Ginger Mayerson
Glen Freddo
Glen Morry
Glenn Fannick
Goran Lukic
Greg Bednarski
Greg Foltz
Greg Loveless
Greg Mailloux
Gregory Annen
Guy Chase
Hae Yuon Kim
Hal Dunn
Hal Jalikeakek
Harlan May
Harry Jones
Harry Karadimas
Heather Coburn-Schill
Heather Jones
Heidi Leinonen
Hunter Boyle
Hurston Prescott
Iain McCarthy
Ian Cameron
Ian Scorrer
Jack Bilson
Jacqueline Celenza
James Gould
James Huston
James Meek
James Steen
James Tullous
James Warner
Jane Tabachnick
Janet Cutrona
Janet LoFurno
Jason Karpf
Jason Lemons
Jason Plansky
Jay Hamacek
Jed Alger
Jeff Babb
Jeff Hendricks
Jeff Kirk

Jeff Sewell
Jeffrey Travis
Jennifer Discoll
Jennifer Ingraham
Jennifer Regelman
Jennifer Shannon
Jennifer Willsey
Jeremy Glesner
Jeremy Sherman
Jerry Martin
Jez Godin
Jill Mazur
Jill Whalen
Jim Buck
Jim Cook
Jim Mattingly
Jim Mauro
Jim Rimmer
Jim Roe
Jo Morris
Joachim Ritschmann
Joe Shields
Joe Tangredi
Joeth Barlas
John Brooks
John Burland
John Cornellier
John Dini
John Driscoll
John Friedman
John Gulliford
John Hiatt
John Lynch
John Mackenzie
John Merritt
John Mielke
John Rodstrom
John Tate
John Trefry
John Webb
Jonathan Sneider
Jonathan Vehar
Joyce Reed
Judi Darnbrough
Judith Plantz
Judy Vorfeld
Julie Ditolla
Julie Power
Julie Swords

Justine Scorrer
Jutta Gardiner
K Hochman
K. Hough
Karen Bojda
Kathryn Purcell
Kathy Felong
Kathy Thompson
Kathy Willhoite
Katie Tang
Katie Walston
Kaye Felgate
Keith Dennis
Ken Banks
Ken Bryson
Ken Thomas
Ken Turner
Kevin DelVecchio
Kevin Dougherty
Kevin Gillogly
Kevin Hewitt
Kevin Johnson
Kevin Kirk
Kieran Dowling
Kris Shepherd
Kristin Arnold
L. David Kingsley
L. Lepori
Lance Smith
Laura Wagner
Laurel Sutton
Lawrence
     Brenninkmeyer
Lee Benjamin
Lee Pennekamp
Leonard Sachs
Leslie Nelson
Linda Breuer
Linda Martin
Lisa Kaiser
Lisa McIntosh
Llew Keller
Lori Schug
Lorraine Jackson
Lovell Fuller
Lyn Laboriel
Lynne Fiero
Lynne Shapiro
Lynne Westphal

Marc Hoopingarner
Margaret Biblis
Margaret Wilson
Marguerita Johnston
Marguerite Savard
Maria Dittrich
Marie Dakin
Marilynn Smith
Mark Feldbauer
Mark Hampton
Mark Metcalf
Mark Schaffer
Mark Schlepphorst
Mark Worden
Mark Wudarski
Marko Bon
Martin Johncox
Mary Gray Rust
Mary Mullins
Mary Parker
Mary Ronan Drew
Matt Baker
Matt Cahill
Matt Constantine
Matt Spera
Max Dieterle
Max Matthews
Mel Carter
Mel O'Leary
Melinda Kinard
Melissa Theil
Michael Brown
Michael Chwastiak
Michael Kotch
Michael Larson
Michael Morris
Michael Richardson
Michael Sims
Michael Taylor
Michael Theil
Michael Troiano
Michael Zuckerman
Michelle Hornsby
Michelle Porter
Mike Boyle
Mike Brehm
Mike Capsambelis
Mike Carpenter
Mike Fratini

Mike Gilmer
Mike Hess
Mike High
Mike Knox
Mike Wheeler
Mike Whitaker
Mike Zraly
Mindy Parsons
Nancy Wells
Nathan Hall
Nicholas Jabro
Nick Catania
Nick Linsalata
Nick Nielsen
Nick Petricevich
Nicole Sherrod
Olivier Stephenson
Pam Greenberg
Pat Kelley
Patricia Bohner
Patricia Bonnstetter
Patrick Kerr
Patrick Vagnier
Patsy Evans
Patty Bonnstetter
Paul Barrett
Paul Casey
Paul Hupkes
Paul LaVigne
Paul Nelson
Paul Nickell
Paul Strandlund
Paula Johnson
Pete Saussy
Peter Cook
Peter Hadley
Peter Vogel
Peter Zanger
Phil Brown
Phil Spray
Phil Wallace
Radhakrishnan Thampi
Ralph Buck
Ralph Calvert

Randall Becker
Randy Sheehan
Ray Griffin
Rebecca Cavanaugh
Renee Thompson
Rhys Wilkins
Richard Beanland
Richard Budd
Richard Curtis
Richard Jasinski
Richie Solomon
Rick Roach
Rob Lawless
Rob Monteleone
Rob Stolper
Robert J. Van Leeuwen
Robert Johnston
Robert McCall
Robin Corpuz
Rod Bartlett
Rodger Beard
Roger Sullivan
Ron Hatcher
Rose Smith
Roxy Gwynn
Roy Bates
Roy Collingwood
Ryan Haberthur
Saman Jebeli-Javan
Samara Romagnola
Samra Jones-Bufkins
Sandie Wilson
Sandra Sims
Sarah Beatty
Sarah Clatterbuck
Sarah Stone
Scott Burge
Scott Dittman
Scott Haddon
Scott Jenkins
Scott Niehaus
Scott Richardson
Serge Masse
Sharon Coates-

Jonasson
Shaun Bartlett
Sheri Kiddy
Sid Djerfi
Signy Freyseng
Sionne Roberts
Srimathi Kannan
Stan Schliening
Stephanie Ethier
Steve Buccola
Steve Daniel
Steve Downing
Steve Floyd
Steve Hannaford
Steve Herz
Steve Kristy
Steve Llanso
Steve Rhodes
Steve Waldner
Steve Wilcox
Steve Witoshkin
Steve Witte
Steve Woodsmall
Steve Woodsmall
Steve Wroblewski
Steven Parrish
Steven Phillips
Steven Whittle
Stu Glazebrook
Sue Edworthy
Sue Gemmell
Sue Lipinski
Sue Pietrowski
Sundaram
    Chandrasekaran
Susan Albright
Susan Lister
Susan Martin
Susan Pietrowski
Susan Rayburn
Susan Walton
Susana Carcasona
Susie Cook
Suzanne Egbert

Suzanne Pietrowski
T.J. Walston
Tami Spinks
Tanya Katz
Ted Arnold
Teresa Henderson
Terry Porter
Thad Bartlett
Thom Menzies
Thomas Golembeski
Thomas King
Thomas Lampros
Thomas Pitre
Tim Blankenhorn
Tim Ewbank
Tim Hall
Tim Kinnel
Tim Wood
Todd Dollinger
Todd Seal
Tom Mackey
Tom McCool
Tom Namtvedt
Tom Stovall
Tony Molinero
Tony Phipps
Trish Sammer
Tsvi Goldstein
Tyrone Slothrop
Valerie Noll
Vanessa Witmer
Vaughan Tyson
Vik Chopra
Vikas Tibrewala
Vince Owens
Volsted Gridban
Vona Van Cleef
Walter Hull
Ward Smith
Will Dixon
Will Duckworth
William Barrett
Wirkman Virkkala